YOUR FIRST YEAR AS

PRINCIPAL:

EVERYTHING YOU NEED TO

KNOW THAT THEY DO NOT

TEACH YOU IN SCHOOL

By Tena Green

YOUR FIRST YEAR AS PRINCIPAL:
EVERYTHING YOU NEED TO KNOW THAT THEY DO NOT TEACH YOU IN SCHOOL

ISBN-13: 978-1-60138-220-7   ISBN-10: 1-60138-220-0

Library of Congress Cataloging-in-Publication Data

Green, Tena, 1960-
  Your first year as a principal : everything you need to know that they
don't teach you in school / by Tena Green.
      p. cm.
  Includes bibliographical references and index.
  ISBN-13: 978-1-60138-220-7 (alk. paper)
  ISBN-10: 1-60138-220-0 (alk. paper)
  1. First year school principals--United States--Handbooks, manuals, etc.
  2. School management and organization--United States--Handbooks, manuals, etc. I. Title.

  LB2831.92.K45 2008
  371.2'012--dc22
                            2008035307

Printed in the United States

Printed on Recycled Paper

We recently lost our beloved pet "Bear," who was not only our best and dearest friend but also the "Vice President of Sunshine" here at Atlantic Publishing. He did not receive a salary but worked tirelessly 24 hours a day to please his parents. Bear was a rescue dog that turned around and showered myself, my wife Sherri, his grandparents Jean, Bob and Nancy and every person and animal he met (maybe not rabbits) with friendship and love. He made a lot of people smile every day.

We wanted you to know that a portion of the profits of this book will be donated to The Humane Society of the United States. *–Douglas & Sherri Brown*

The human-animal bond is as old as human history. We cherish our animal companions for their unconditional affection and acceptance. We feel a thrill when we glimpse wild creatures in their natural habitat or in our own backyard.

Unfortunately, the human-animal bond has at times been weakened. Humans have exploited some animal species to the point of extinction.

The Humane Society of the United States makes a difference in the lives of animals here at home and worldwide. The HSUS is dedicated to creating a world where our relationship with animals is guided by compassion. We seek a truly humane society in which animals are respected for their intrinsic value, and where the human-animal bond is strong.

Want to help animals? We have plenty of suggestions. Adopt a pet from a local shelter, join The Humane Society and be a part of our work to help companion animals and wildlife. You will be funding our educational, legislative, investigative and outreach projects in the U.S. and across the globe.

Or perhaps you'd like to make a memorial donation in honor of a pet, friend or relative? You can through our Kindred Spirits program. And if you'd like to contribute in a more structured way, our Planned Giving Office has suggestions about estate planning, annuities, and even gifts of stock that avoid capital gains taxes.

Maybe you have land that you would like to preserve as a lasting habitat for wildlife. Our Wildlife Land Trust can help you. Perhaps the land you want to share is a backyard—that's enough. Our Urban Wildlife Sanctuary Program will show you how to create a habitat for your wild neighbors.

So you see, it's easy to help animals. And The HSUS is here to help.

2100 L Street NW • Washington, DC 20037
202-452-1100 • www.hsus.org

DEDICATION

This book is dedicated to all the great principals without whom this book would not be possible, to Bill Hall, Dr. DiPatri, and especially the great principals who left a lasting impression on my life, Mr. Carl Howard and Mr. Bruce Kimbrell.

CONTENTS

FOREWORD

———

I remember walking into "my" building my first day as a new principal. I had spent many years as an educator in the public schools of New York City, both as a teacher and as an assistant principal, but this was different. After a rigorous interview process, and after waiting for an entire summer, I was informed that I had been selected for the position.

I walked into an office and was greeted not by a secretary, but a fax machine working overtime spewing out reams of paper from both the superintendent's office and the central board of education. I spent the day reading through the memos and directives and opening the mail that had accumulated over the summer.

The next day I met the faculty. They were a group of educators who looked upon me as the "enemy" because they had an allegiance to another person in the school who did not get the position. Could I win them over? The students were to enter the building the next day and it seemed like nothing was ready. Was curriculum in place? Were student programs ready? Were all of the teachers hired and given their proper assignments? Were the classrooms inviting? Was the support staff in place? What about new students who were showing up to be enrolled at the school? How should I respond to the fax machine that did not quit?

In all the classes I took while studying to become an administrator, there was nothing taught which could have prepared me for the experiences I had during the first weeks and months of being a new principal.

Did I survive? I'm happy to say yes. Could my life have been easier if I had some preliminary guidelines to help me through those hectic beginnings? Absolutely.

It is with these memories in place that I am happy to be able to recommend Tena Green's new book, *Your First Year as a Principal: Everything You Need to Know That They Don't Teach You in School.*

This is a wonderful book written by someone viewing the school and a principal's job not as an educator, but as someone who has been in schools in a variety of roles, working with teachers, students, and administrators.

Newly appointed principals enter into their positions with a vision of where they want their school to be in a few years, building on past strengths and eliminating any areas of concern. The chapters in this book are presented in a clear and concise way that will assist a new principal in achieving these goals.

As the head administrator of a school, what are your priorities? Hopefully, your main priority will be the students in your building. Everything you do should fall under the heading, "Is this good for my students?" Can your students answer the following questions: What am I learning? Why am I learning this? How can I use it?

While the best interests of our students are the first priority, how do we deal with the myriad of other responsibilities that we, as principals, incur?

As a principal, you know you have to deal with students, faculty, guidance counselors, school aides, secretaries, and building support teams such as custodial and cafeteria workers and the school nurse; however, the job does not end inside the school walls. The principal is also an integral part of the community – dealing with parents, civic organizations, local businesses, and cultural institutions, just to name a few. There are also demands from the district superintendent, local school board, and state and government departments of education. The principal is a master juggler, wearing different hats all at the same time. What about the personal life of the principal? How does one balance the needs of the position with the need for a personal life?

This book will give newly appointed principals, and even those who have been in the position longer, valuable insight into the difficult, but ultimately rewarding, job as a school leader.

The chapters inform the reader about a variety of important issues confronting new principals. They detail a principal's responsibilities, how to assess what needs to be done in the school, how to effectively make change, and how to insure the change becomes institutionalized. The final chapter contains an engaging conversation with successful principals. Thoughtful and topical questions are posed and answered in a way that provides valuable tools for the novice school leader.

Best of luck to you as you embark on your new journey. Your position is an important one, which potentially can have a profound effect on your school, community and, most importantly, your students. Keep this book with you and refer to it often throughout your years as a school leader as it is a valuable resource.

Ira Shankman, BS, MA, MEd
Music and Performing Arts Professions
New York University

INTRODUCTION

Other than my father, there was one man who had a remarkable impact on my life, and that was my principal, Carl Howard. Mr. Howard was a big man, his size alone intimidating, but more importantly he was a man who left a lasting impression. When I was asked why he made such an impression, I realized there was not one reason but many. It was not just his gentle nature, his kindness or his firm but understanding authority, it was also his ability to laugh with his students and faculty, his fairness in discipline, his obvious regret at having to use that discipline, and his sincere caring for his students and staff. All these qualities made my school years an everlasting memory, and it was due to one great man.

As a student there was never a thought given to what my principal's duties were, even when he paddled me for smoking in the bathroom. As a parent my focus was on my children's education, not the principal's responsibility for that education. When I worked as a teacher's assistant, intervention specialist, and substitute secretary, I caught a mere glimpse of the enormity of the principal's job. It was an eye opener to look back on my 30-plus years of work from these different perspectives, and to have witnessed the importance of the principal's job and its necessity. For all these reasons I decided to try to help first-year principals as they struggle to define their place as leaders. My experience comes from many different vantage points, and I have tremendous respect for principals and the challenges they face.

The realization of the principal's influence on students made me ask, "Why?" "What is expected of today's principals?" and "What it is like to carry such weight, especially for first-year principals?"

I have learned that a good principal's main objective is to meet the needs of his or her students; to guide them, help them, discipline them and encourage them no matter what the situation. A worthy leader brings all his or her talents, not just to the office, but to every hallway and room of the school. The students will love and respect you as a leader and you will make a difference. You have chosen a noble cause; one with tremendous impact on numerous lives.

In researching the responsibilities of these leaders many questions came to mind. Unless it is a new institution and you are the first in the door, someone tread the path before you. What groundwork did they lay? What impression did they leave behind? How do you follow their course, or do you begin new groundwork with a different path? When do you implement change? How do you handle a conflict with an irate parent, teacher, or student? How do you react in an explosive situation such as the alleged lesbian molestation case in New Jersey between the 17-year-old student and teacher, Erica Umosella? How will you prepare teachers for new curriculum? How will you discipline your students? Who will be your mentor?

The questions are endless, the answers priceless.

In *Your First Year as a Principal: Everything You Need to Know that They Do Not Teach You in School,* we will answer these questions and more. We will speak with veteran principals and tap into their wisdom. We also will speak to entry-year principals who have just recently lived through what you are now experiencing. Principals, like teachers, are taught steps to handle certain situations. Most leaders who enter an educational institution have a game plan, but the truth is they find their game plan does not always work. Because no one knows what they will do in any given situation until they are standing in the thick of it, we will share with you suggestions, advice, jokes, sad stories, happy endings, and insights into what you might expect.

This book is by no means a step-by-step guide to tell you how to handle your job. All incidents vary, and one must take action — or not — accordingly. This book is merely a reference tool, a piece of mind you can hold in your hand to use for direction and much needed sanity. It is to let you know that you are not alone. In addition it is a testimony of respect to remind you that what you are doing is recognized as a work of significant magnitude. It is there to reassure you that there are those of us out there who are cheering and thanking you for prioritizing the education of our children. It is because of leaders such as yourself that many children grow up to be contributing resources, confident adults, and outstanding examples for their own children.

To those of you who strive to make all that transpires and transforms in our schools every year, I would like to say with sincere gratitude, "Thank you."

1
ASSESSING THE SITUATION

While in college you studied a long list of duties including how to become a principal; everything from directing maintenance of the school building to implementing a new curriculum. What the list did not detail was how complicated and trying it can be to succeed in this chosen and most important profession, or how overwhelming the job can be, especially in the beginning.

School has not yet started, so this is a good time to get a feel for your new home away from home. Walk the halls, stroll the school grounds, look around every classroom, the gymnasium and lunchroom, the custodian's room, the boiler room, and every nook and cranny. Observe the characteristics of this building, and listen to what it tells you. Thousands of young lives will pass through these halls, and you will have an effect on every one of them. Study the school's layout and know it by heart before the year begins. Study the school's history, the culture of the area, the community and its members' ideas, expectations, future dreams for their children's education, and past disappointments.

In order to succeed as a good leader you must assess the educational institution in which you are now in charge, and then create a strategy that will help you accomplish success in achieving your goals. You have the job. Now it is up to you to wear all the assorted hats that you will find waiting for you in the closet of your office. Every day you will wear a number of those hats, and except for other principals, you will become more diverse than anyone you know. The first step to making your school all it should and can be is up to you and you alone. It is one of the easier steps of the millions you will take throughout your career.

We will begin assessing your situation with a glance at a few of the procedural duties in which you are expected to achieve success. By doing this, you may want to take notes on which areas you need to study; decide what your weak areas are, and the steps needed to improve or learn from them. Due to the nature of the following list, we are going to call these "Tactical Tasks."

- Implement educational programs and curriculums development.

- Put into operation developmental curriculums for students.

- Observe teaching in the classroom and apply instructional strategies.

- Understand legislature and litis of your state, district and community.

- Mandate and disperse monies where needed.

- Establish public relations with the community.

- Coordinate an auxiliary support system or maintain the one in place.

- Hire, fire, retain, promote, and dismiss personnel.

- Provide resources and training for your educators.

- Coordinate school activities.

- Assess student accomplishment and implement strategies to improve student achievement.

- Create a safe school environment.

- Set high standards for student learning.

- Be responsible and self-reliant.

- Continue to pursue high levels of learning.

- Overlook student achievement and maintain continuous improvement.

- Maintain discipline standards.

At first glance this list may not seem overwhelming, but in total it is a large undertaking. This list is merely a fraction of what a good leader needs to do. So step back and assess the situation, define the position and set goals.

When you are hired to be a principal, the normal steps are to begin planning for the school year immediately. You may be lucky and find that the previous principal did some of the planning for you, but even if this is the case, you must be sure to review these plans and create your own version of what needs to be done. If you are hired in the middle of the school year, you will find that things will move along without much, if any, input, but you should observe everything possible and take notes for the following year's changes.

During the months before school begins, look over the students' achievement records, check out the local assessments that are used to report student progress, and meet your staff. After school resumes be sure to revisit the staff in-house. Assessing student records and achievements will give you an idea of success or failure. Is it the curriculum? Are the teachers succeeding or failing? If there are weak areas it may be that the student is the problem. But the only way to find out is to observe the class and study the teaching methods and tools that are in use. Observing classes will come later, but for now, you must learn all you can on your own. Summer is a good time to assess the buildings and schedule any modifications necessary. When these tasks are done, or at least under way, it is time to review the budget and note where funds have been spent. Much of the budget, unfortunately, is needed in the classrooms, and you cannot budget according to necessity without observing class time; keep this in mind.

When teachers and staff return to school for the coming year you will need a checklist. This list should have names of people to speak with. If you are lucky, this register will include the names of all your teachers, coaches, counselors, custodians, secretaries, food service workers, media, and parents. It is where the assessment of the inside workings of your educational institution begins. It also is the beginning of building relationships with your personnel. When school resumes you will want to walk the halls; watching, observing, learning, introducing yourself, and getting to know the ins and outs of students and teachers, and the atmosphere that surrounds you. This activity has a simple goal — make yourself visible. It is the best way to establish yourself as the authority figure, but more importantly, it is the best way to reassure your students and staff that you are accessible.

Besides the Tactical Tasks, there are other less procedural duties that you are expected to perform. These duties are more personal, and tend to be that of developing and maintaining relationships with the community, personnel, and students of your institution. These undertakings may not have the same significance for some administrators, but principals should make note that without the success of the following partial list of duties, the Tactical Tasks have a lesser chance of being successful. We are going to title this list "Necessary Elements."

- Establish good relationships with all students and teachers.

- Ascertain excellent standing with parents and community.

- Help set up and maintain a parent/teacher committee.

- Attend after school functions.

- Provide time for students, teachers, and parents.

- Lead and support your teachers.

- Supply resources for your personnel.

- Show interest in your student's needs and accomplishments.

- Promptly reply to letters, e-mail, and phone calls.

- Support librarians, coaches, staff, counselors, and other personnel.

- Meet with representatives of community organizations.

- Be involved with students' emotional welfare.

- Be visible to students and staff.

- Recognize and reward teacher achievement.

- Be supportive of school culture.

- Attend ceremonies and affirm student achievement.

- Be a role model.

The two lists we have reviewed are by no means an exaggeration. If anything, they are short when compared to the true and continuing lists of duties a principal must face. Be assured, you can achieve these tasks and many more. Many great leaders have walked the halls before you and succeeded, and you can, too. You can achieve your goals, and become the kind of principal that will leave a positive impact on those you guide.

> *"If students, staff, and parents feel safe at our school, then everything else should fall into place."*
>
> **Barry Pichard, Principal**
> Sunrise Elementary School
> Palm Bay, Florida

A Principal's Priorities

When you were hired for this central position, the superintendent and school board informed you whether their school was not successful and what they wanted to accomplish, or they informed you of their success and let you know that it was now up to you to keep the achievement intact. What they did not tell you was how to accomplish either goal; whether it was in achieving success or maintaining it.

Now that the job is yours, the weight of countless responsibilities sits on your shoulders. You may feel slightly intimidated, and possibly afraid.

While interviewing principals for this book, it did not take long to realize that there were some answers that were similar. The one question that stands out in my mind is, "What are your top personal priorities as a principal?" In reading over the answers from principals across the country I realized the answer was the same from each of them. The "safety of the students" is a top personal priority of our principals in the schools today.

This priority made me stop and think about the tremendous responsibility you will carry in your role as principal. Parents sometimes think it is hard to be responsible for one, two, three, or even four kids, but how about 200, or 300, or 500 students? This is a responsibility you are constantly aware of and few parents think of until the unimaginable happens. Principals all over the country are concerned about this possibility on a daily basis.

Although parents read the headlines in the newspapers, they tend to believe that much of the "news" is hype. They turn a blind eye to some of these reports knowing the media have become nothing more than glorified, gossip columns and propaganda pushers. Then there are the times we see or read about school shootings, our blind eye focuses on the headlines as we read every word of the article, and silently pray that this will never happen in our schools.

When veteran principals verify that "safety" is their top priority, first-year principals should take note. The possible threat of violence erupting in your school is a concern you must learn to deal with. When asked about the possibility of violence in schools, all new and veteran principals agree it is a concern for which they and the school boards have thoroughly prepared.

Parenting and education are the two most important factors in determining a child's future; and the principal's job is second only to a parent's. This fact alone is more than enough to weigh heavily on a principal's shoulders, especially a first-year principal. There is much more at stake than the mere future of an infinite number of students. Your responsibility spreads from inside the school to beyond the doors of your establishment. Once your students leave your hallowed halls much of the end result of their adulthood rests with you. How they are as learners, educators, and examples for others, has been a part of your responsibility as well as their parents. If they become contributing resources it can affect your school's community, your state, your country, and in some way, the whole world. But do not panic.

The fact that you took this job indicates that you have a sincere interest in education and the welfare of our students. Your leadership is the foundation on which they will bud, bloom, grow, flower, and flourish. Because of your passion you will touch many souls and leave an everlasting impressions. It is up to you whether that impression is good or bad.

The question now is what are your priorities? The job is yours but the question remains; what are you going to do with this institution? If you recall the two lists earlier in this chapter, "Tactical Tasks" and "Necessary Elements," you will remember your responsibilities. There are certain tasks you must do because it is in the best interest of the students, and also, because it is in the fine print of your contract. Other tasks, however, should be accomplished to achieve success in the areas spelled out in your job description. It is the way to a much smoother road, and a happier student body, staff, and principal.

Your first priority must be your students and personnel. You may wonder, why the teachers? Their job may seem to be clear-cut, but in order to assess the situation in your educational institution you must have your teachers' help. They are invaluable resources for the following needs:

- Teach students and help them achieve academic success

- Inform principal of student performance

- Inform principal regarding students' emotional welfare and safety

- Inform principal of failing curriculums; develop new curriculums

- Help assess and implement new ideas and strategies

- Help with time-consuming tasks: develop and lead organizations, attending meetings, perform public relations duties

- Help boost morale of students and other staff members.

This list demonstrates how important it is to establish good relations with your teachers. Without their support your job will be impossible to perform. The best way to support your teachers is to let them know you respect their positions, prove to them that you will be there when they need you, and take their input seriously. To assure your teachers try the following:

- Talk to them one on one and let them know you value their positions and opinions

- Ask directly for their input

- Ask for their ideas, thoughts, and personal opinions on anything they feel needs to be noticed, rectified, or changed

- Let them know your door is always open

- Communicate that they are invaluable, and that you need their help and support

- Take notes and follow up with them, even if it means disappointment about a change you cannot make

- Consider writing up a questionnaire for future reference

- Ask for a list of needs

- Assure them that you will do everything possible to make their job easier.

While we have been talking about the importance of your teachers and students, you may have forgotten something else that is extremely important. Where would the teachers and students be without you?

In assessing your situation, you have now realized your first resource for success is you. Yes, you. You are the leader of the institution. You are the one invaluable resource your teachers need to help produce successful students. Without you their job is impossible. Without you the students cannot succeed, and move to the next level of their life.

The second realization is that in order for you to succeed as a leader, you need a good working relationship with your teachers, and successful students. A successful educational establishment is no different from the hallways you will now walk — traffic flows two ways. To begin your school year on a positive note — ideas and support must also flow two ways.

You are assessing and learning about your school. Your teachers can give you more information than necessary, but be warned, it is still the beginning of the year. Do not barge into the school with a list of changes that stretches across the football field. Do not demand drastic changes that you want implemented within the first week. This kind of action causes poor attitudes and distrust, and it makes you look like a greenhorn or an idiotic dictator.

Another word of caution — be careful making promises. If you make promises you cannot keep, you will cause major damage to what could be resourceful relationships. Take all requests seriously, and give each of them careful consideration; but never promise a result, immediate or otherwise. Even if you must refuse a request, follow up with a discussion and explanation. Diplomacy means everything in your position.

In reviewing student success and failure from the previous year and taking notes of your teachers input on the subjects you need to know and thoroughly understand, you now have assessed a large and important part of your situation. You should feel good in knowing that this necessary step leads you to a much smoother path, not only this year, but for the coming year as well. Unfortunately, it is just another small step in achieving success.

Previous Footsteps and Mentors

One important factor your professors might possibly have overlooked is the previous leader that you will have to follow. This factor may cause you much joy and relief, or create untold problems in your new job. We are going to look at these two scenarios and discover ways to deal with each one, because ready or not, one of these two possibilities is now your situation.

If you are fortunate you have now discovered the previous leader of your school left you in a good position. If this is the case you might consider yourself lucky. You may soon come to realize, however, that this is not necessarily the case. A great leader leaves big shoes to fill, and it is possible that your teachers, staff, students, administrators, and even the community may see you lacking in leadership skills before you get started. This is now a turnaround; the community and populace of your school will be assessing you.

Before you sat in that principal's chair, you felt relieved that you were following an exceptional leader. After all he left an establishment that was running smoothly, and considered a success. Then the day came when you entered the office, took a seat in his revered chair, and realized something different than what you expected. Just between us you can admit it; you are new and inexperienced, and you are scared to death that you will not be able to fill his shoes. Rest easy. It is all right to feel intimidated, and it is perfectly understandable. Before you decide you might have made a mistake in taking the job, take comfort in knowing that all first-year principals feel the same at the beginning of their career — regardless who they follow. The best advice one can give a new principal in this situation is to remember the students and staff are mourning an important loss. Understand and be patient, show that you respect their feelings, and know that respect only comes with time.

> *"Make a friend with another administrator and be able to share experiences."*
>
> **John Redd, Principal**
> Bellevue Junior High
> Bellevue, Ohio

As we have already verified, the overwhelming tasks you are required to perform on a daily basis are almost limitless. You are responsible for everything from instructional leadership to managing day-to-day activities. Your school's previous leader might be a good mentor, one who can give advice and feedback. With today's schools facing a reduction in budgets, diminishing resources, and constant social changes, you will want to use all the resources available. A good mentor is a priceless supply of information, feedback, moral support, and understanding. A mentor is someone you will want to have accessible. Most states are implementing mentoring programs for teachers and principals. Hawaii and the Pacific Region have institutions principals can call for consultation. Ohio has redesigned a new program for entry-year principals which has two unique elements; an induction program for first-year-principals, and a mentoring component for principals and assistant principals. In Ohio there are two associations principals can turn to for help in their efforts to improve education: The Ohio Association of Elementary School Administrators (OAESA) and The Ohio Association of Secondary School Administrators (OASSA). All states offer some type of association to help improve education and the quality of school leadership.

The following states the OAESA mission:

- To bring about a more complete understanding of the objectives of the elementary and middle school administrators

- To work for the continuous improvement of Ohio's elementary and middle level schools

- To cooperate with organizations who share mutual interest in promoting the cause of quality education.

The OASSA mission is "to provide high standards of leadership through professional development, political astuteness, legislative influence, positive public relations, and collaboration with related organizations."

As you can see from these few examples, good leadership for our children's education is imperative. The job of leading in an educational environment is stressful; therefore, guidance, advice, and feedback are just some of the qualities a mentor can provide. Another priceless resource a mentor can bring to the table is being able to understand your position and your responsibilities. A mentor is a confidante and a good listener, and can help alleviate stress.

Following an ineffective principal can be cause for major hurdles and headaches. Because of bad leadership you may experience trust issues from staff, students, and the community. The curriculums most likely will be outdated, tools for teaching practically nonexistent, and the building may be falling down around your head. In order to repair the damage left by the previous principal, you must understand it will take time. On your entry as the new principal, you may even experience reactions as severe as hostility.

Another possible scenario is facing resentment from staff members who were contenders for the job you now hold. You may be able to win some over by adding them to your various teams; acknowledging their talents and using their abilities to your advantage for the betterment of your school. Others may never be won over, and this is a fact you may have to accept.

If you are following a bad leader your first approach may be to tap into your resources. Budgets may be limited, but your teachers can and do teach without state-of-the-art equipment. The solution is not the software or technology but the people. Your people will deliver solutions and ideas on how to work around the budget to make your institution a success in educating the students. Good teachers want the students to get a good education. If they know their leader wants the same, they will be more than happy to help you achieve this goal.

An important realization is that a good leader should have the ability to lead. It is not necessary for you to take on all the responsibility alone. It is imperative, however, that you let your personnel know that you not only need help but you welcome it. Many times a new principal may take a job without knowing the one who left; the previous principal may be one who refused to help others or refused to allow others to help him or her.

You may feel somewhat isolated and lonely at the beginning, but as noted previously, there are things you can do to solidify the relationships you wish to have with your staff and students. Remember, it is important as a leader to be seen. You will have no help nor receive any respect if you hide in your office sitting behind your desk waiting for the end of the day. You must be seen by students and staff in order to define who you are and why you are there.

A school which is haunted with the lingering shadow of a less-than-effective leader may take more time to organize. On the other hand once your personnel and students realize your good intentions you most likely will find them sincere in their welcome.

The benefits of having a good mentor should be mentioned once again. You are now in a position that will seem, at the least, overwhelming and at most, impossible. A good mentor can help relieve your certainty that this job is a lost cause, and he or she also can help you maintain a much-needed positive attitude. Imagine making a list of the qualities in principals you have known. Those principals should be, at the very least: honest, fair, dependable, trustworthy, organized, calm, consistent, supportive, and energetic.

Using Your Staff

With your teachers in mind, if you look back to the "Tactical Tasks" and "Necessary Elements" lists of procedural duties you must accomplish, you will notice the value of good teachers. In implementing educational programs and curriculums development there is no one who can better inform you of what is needed in each classroom. Teachers are the ones who put into operation the developmental curriculums for your students. When you observe teaching, and suggest instructional strategies, your teachers apply those strategies. The educators inform you of classroom needs just as the librarian informs you of the library needs. All this information helps you decide the best way to disperse the budget. Staff also can help you establish public relations with the community, take coordinating roles in auxiliary support systems and school activities, and ease some of the weight that rests on your shoulders. Your personnel can keep you up to date on student achievement and student welfare.

Without support and lending hands from your teachers and staff you will have a hard time establishing good relationships with your students and their parents. Having a teacher volunteer to represent the school administration, and attend parent and teacher committee meetings is an important resource. With all the responsibilities you will be stretched thin. So it is a good idea to have a few reliable teachers to call on to attend school functions when you can not.

Your staff can help you out by providing time for your students and parents. They also can keep you informed of any student needs, accomplishments, conflicts or emotional concerns.

If you have a high-quality food-service leader you will have one less challenge to worry about. If the food menu is in good hands you can concentrate on more important matters. A first-rate counselor will tell you if there is a problem you should be aware of. If you know your staff is capable of handling pressing issues you will be comfortable knowing you can put your time to other matters until you are needed. Good coaches will take care of sports needs and players so you do not have to look over their shoulders to make sure things are as they should be. Mrs. Smith, the fantastic English teacher you inherited, will be attending all the PTO meetings allowing you the much-needed time to go over those new test categories the state is implementing next year. The custodian will be more than happy to do a good job for you, and your students for no reason other than the respect he or she is given. Your secretaries will be your friends because you recognize their hard work. And the bus drivers will like you because you take the time to talk to them and inquire if all is running smoothly.

Never forget that parents, volunteers, and student teachers are important. If you take the time to speak with them and show respect, they will be supportive and helpful.

Where are we going with this information? Quality personnel are imperative and they are a fine resource for a good principal. Great leaders are not afraid to let others lead. Brilliant leaders search for others to lead. Using your staff in this way is not only beneficial for your time but also for your peace of mind. One thing you must be aware of in using your staff for leading roles is that you must never assume everything is going fine. You must take the time to meet with your chosen leaders; take the time to go over all information available about the decisions being considered; and you must sit in on meetings occasionally to stay on top of situations.

By using your staff appropriately you will have more time to give to other matters. After all, you are needed for things as simple as standing in the hallways during class change to discovering resources and tools for your teachers. As you can see your staff is invaluable in helping to lighten the load of your unyielding responsibilities. It is in your personal interest, as well as that of your educational institution, to create a good relationship with your staff and use them where needed.

A Clear View

We have discussed only some of the places you need to look in order to assess your institution. There are so many responsibilities that one must make a list of priorities, and stick to that list to avoid burnout before the year even begins. So far you have studied past student achievement to gain an idea of where curriculums, and/or the teachers may be succeeding or failing. You have plans to sit in during classroom time to get an overview of your teachers' abilities, disciplinary actions, how the curriculum is being used, and decide what, if anything, needs to change. You have a list of all personnel so that you may talk with each of them, one on one, to determine what their needs are, and to discover your strongest links for future committee leaders. You know that the best way to overcome a lingering shadow left by a previous leader is to gain the respect of your staff and the students, and give them back the respect they deserve. You know the importance of a good mentor and have begun looking for one or have found one. You have an idea of good sources for tools and training for teachers, and plan to deal with these issues as soon as you have a list of needs. We have verified the "Tactical Tasks" you must accomplish, but more importantly, the "Necessary Elements" that you will need to implement in order to succeed. The overall view is becoming clear and once the year has begun you will be better prepared to find the gaps that exist on the path from Point A to Point B.

2
THE GAP ANALYSIS

Now that school has begun and you have assessed the situation, how far is it from Point A, where your educational institution is, to Point B, where your educational institution should be? Some of you may be wondering if this is a trick question simply because now you have assessed where the school is and where it should be, and you feel even more overwhelmed than you did when you first sat behind the desk. Rest assured this is not a trick question. The solutions will vary for each of you; therefore, there is no set answer. Although this may be comforting to some it may be disconcerting for others.

In determining where you are and where you want to be, you need a course of action. First, you need a course.

Investigating the reasons why your school is not where it needs to be can lead to some disturbing answers. When the students are failing, or falling behind in their studies, the teachers are failing in their job. If the teachers are failing, the principal is failing as a leader. The question then becomes, why? In order to establish the "why," a principal accepts the responsibility of looking at the curriculums of the school, sits in during class time to evaluate teaching methods, and studies the community to search for better-suited curriculums. Also, an outstanding leader will take the time to learn something about each individual student.

You may be relieved to find your institution is having problems because a portion of the student population is Hispanic, and English is their second language. You may have discovered you have no Spanish-speaking teachers. The solution for this problem is relatively simple; find new curriculums to alleviate the language barrier, hire teachers with Spanish-speaking capabilities, and follow-up with a study of the community and its future needs; implement extra curriculums that will be suitable. What if your school is made up of English-speaking students in a middle-income neighborhood with low scores on state tests and academia? How do you find the problem, and how do you implement a solution?

You have looked at the state test results, and found the scores are average or below. You then checked the students' academic records but found they are lacking in many areas. It is no surprise that students score low on state standardized tests as well as in the classroom. However, how can students score average on state tests but poorly in the classrooms? It could be that the teachers have been teaching for the state tests. According to some studies, schools teaching for state tests were a common problem; a knee-jerk reaction to demands for test results to be higher. I witnessed this firsthand when I worked for the local schools. This is not something a good leader would have his or her teachers do. A study of schools that led the way in standardized tests found that principals who were good leaders were more focused on what was best for their students; not what was best for good test results. These principals took what they were already doing for student achievement and added what was necessary to help students achieve good test results. The bottom line is that the best leaders keep a perspective and their priorities in order.

If scores are low in academia as well as state testing, the first place to look is the classroom. It could be that the teachers are not doing their job correctly, doing it poorly, or have no tools with which to teach. This deduction leads us to the dreaded problem of the bad teacher; better known as the bad apple.

There can be numerous reasons for low student achievement, but once you discover what the problems are you must find solutions. Sometimes the solution may be one that will take time to turn around. Sometimes the problem may be simple, but the solution may not be simple. Either way, it is your job as leader to assess, analyze, close the gap, measure the success or failure of the implemented solutions, and give an outlook to your superiors. It simply is up to you to correct the problems.

When one thinks in terms of the problem becoming "my problem," it becomes somewhat clearer and easier to correct, even when it calls for doing something undesirable; which brings us back to the bad apple.

If the answer to your institution's problem is a need of teaching tools, you can access the budget, and start finding resources for your teachers. If your teachers are not teaching correctly or teaching poorly but show integrity, a desire to improve, and the potential to do so, you can facilitate professional development services. There are numerous seminars and classes to help teachers improve their abilities. That leaves us with one premise that brings about the ultimate question — do you have a bad teacher on your hands?

When you are barraged with angry phone calls, visits from parents, and witness poor teaching firsthand, the only thing left to do is to deal with the problem directly. As a leader you must keep in mind that a student who has a weak teacher for a year will fall behind his or her peers. A student who has more than one bad teacher may never catch up. If this is not enough to convince you to force your hand as a principal then you might want to consider an alternative: removing the student or creating improvement plans for the teacher. If possible, the easiest solution is to place the student in another classroom. Why not just fire the teacher? This subject is explored in detail later in this chapter and again in Chapter Five.

In assessing the situation, you may have found a discipline problem in your institution. The discipline of students is mainly up to the teacher; they are the ones who manage the classrooms. The last resort, however, is sending the misbehaving student to the principal. The best way to handle discipline problems is to stop the tribulations before they end up in the principal's office. Discipline can be a touchy subject at best, and sometimes it is difficult to find a set rule to use for a solution. Some schools insist on using assertive discipline. Although this may work for some teachers, it does not work for others. Yet, it is not the rule of discipline being used that poses the problem, it is the teacher.

Mrs. Beresta, a wonderful teacher I had the pleasure to work with as a teacher's assistant, was a natural when it came to disciplining her students. If she had a student who insisted on acting out, she would approach the student and quietly speak with him or her about the behavior. If need be, she would take the student into the hallway to have a private conversation about the issues bothering the student. Seldom did a student have to be sent to the principal's office. On the other hand, we had a teacher who was the opposite. Mr. Waltin would scream at a misbehaving student. He even went so far as to manhandle a few. The last straw was when he pushed one young man against the wall. The problem was not the form of discipline chosen by the school board but obviously the teacher's personal choice in how to handle disciplining the students. Mrs. Beresta's solution was to know her students individually and handle them accordingly. Most students behaved well in Mrs. Beresta's class, and I still believe it was due to mutual respect.

When observing a classroom it is better to enter unannounced. This is the only way you will see the true interaction of teacher and students. The chance to observe with no warning will be short lived, so you must observe the potential problems and solutions within the first few seconds upon entering the room. You need to keep a log of everything that happens, whether approaching the problem or giving credit, for reference when evaluations occur. We will expand on discipline and dealing with conflict more in Chapter Five.

Curriculums and tools for teachers are imperative in finding a course to arrive at Point B. In some states, administrators in school district offices oversee curriculums and direct subject area programs. These administrators supervise instructional coordinators and curriculum specialists. In many cases administrators have transferred primary responsibility for programs to the principals. Principals are now accountable for students meeting national, state, and local academic standards. This adds to the list of responsibilities, and is a major problem for principals; most principals spend the majority of their time attending to management, and conflict. Again, your best resource for choosing the best curriculums and implementation tools are your teachers. After observing classrooms, speak with your teachers about what they feel would enhance their teaching skills, and student achievements.

It is easy to discover if the institution's problems rests with a bad teacher. It gets a bit harder when you enter the zone of the "Necessary Elements." A perfect example is looking at your individual students. This is extremely time consuming but imperative in knowing what is missing in your school. For instance, you may know what their test scores are, but do you know what kind of adult they will be? The bigger question is simple, will they be contributing adults? If not, there are more problems in your school than those readily visible at first glance.

Granted, there are many students who come from broken or abusive homes, their foundations never solid. The groundwork with which the teachers had to expand was not what one would consider a good start. If you are running a stable, smooth, educational, encouraging, and safe school, there is a much better chance for those students to find their way; especially with the help and guidance of you and your staff. The emotional welfare of your students is in your hands If you see students who need emotional support, it is up to you and your personnel to make sure you do what you can to help them.

In the last two chapters we discussed some possible problems and solutions for your institution. Take a glance at this list of problems and continue.

- Teaching for state standardized tests.

- Badly chosen curriculums based on community needs.

- Possibility of a bad apple.

- School discipline.

- Curriculums.

- Previous leader.

- Relationships with teachers.

- Proper use of staff.

Finding the problems is relatively simple. Finding solutions can be extremely trying and sometimes impossible.

Where to Go From Here

You have assessed and analyzed your institution now, but what is your personal vision of where you want to take your school? We are not talking about the school's mission statement, but your own personal vision. You know what curriculum needs are, what the teachers would like to see in their classrooms, what the nation, state, and district want in student achievement. The missing link is your personal preference for your students.

A wake-up call that some first-year principals tend to overlook is the fact that your personnel, students, and community will know what is most important to you by your focus. For example, if a good relationship with your students and teachers is a top priority, you will not convince anyone of this fact if you spend all your time in your office doing paperwork.

You have assessed the preliminary, checked the structure of the building, talked with your teachers, looked over student achievement, assessed the curriculums, and looked for resources that may be needed in the near future. You are now waiting to sit in on your teacher's class time to evaluate how they teach, and if they have the tools they need to do so. You will then take the time to get to know your students individually, not just on paper. You will meet and greet the parents on opening night or at the teacher-parent conference, talk with your kitchen staff, get to know your custodians, learn about each extracurricular activity that takes place inside your building, know who your best teachers are, and have an idea of who your worst teachers might be. You will be sure to have an appointment to meet your PTO president, the media, the academic booster president, the alumni president, the mayor and president of city council, and many more people who will make your school tick like a fine clock. Yet the job is nowhere near done.

A Contagious Vision

Each principal is a unique individual. Each has his idea of how a school should be run and how it should be done. But do you have a vision of what you want your school base to be? Do you have an idea of what you want your students to take with them when they receive that diploma and walk out the doors as a student for the last time? Do you even know what your vision is?

> *Vision is the act or power of anticipating that which will or may come to be. It is also described as a vivid, imaginative conception or anticipation.*

If you had to guarantee a new student something that he or she would leave your school with what would it be? In order to obtain your vision and before tackling a task, you should ask yourself these questions: Will this task I am about to do get us closer to my vision? Will this task help me stand behind my promise to the students that they will leave this institution with a good, solid education? You must know what your vision is for your school before you can make it happen, and that is just the first step.

To determine your vision you should ask yourself some questions: What drives me? What brought me to choose this career? When I chose this path what were my reasons? What did I believe I could do for an educational institution?

It was your passion for giving students a good education that brought you to this point in your life. Think back and recall the thoughts you had then, because it was those beliefs, those dreams, that got you here. And it was those thoughts and dreams that will get you and your school to Point B.

You now know what is expected of you by your new line-up of administration, your community, your personnel, and to some extent, your students. But to arrive at Point B, you have to know what you expect of yourself. You have to know not only what you expect of yourself, but also what you expect of your staff. Whatever it is — that is your vision.

Once you know what your vision is, what your school problems are, and what tools and training are needed to get to Point B, you must come up with a strategy to make it happen. Unfortunately, saying it can be much easier than doing it.

You are the only one who can come up with your unique, individual vision, but someone who might be able to help you do so would be your mentor. Being able to talk to someone who knows what you are experiencing and what you mean when you say, "I want my students to feel they are special," is like having a second brain to work for you. This mentor can help you put into words what you feel but cannot say. The mentor can help you define your passion, your dream for your institution, and your desire for your students' future.

A principal's vision for his or her school is more than just a dream; it is a possibility. Think about that statement for just a minute. Your vision is not just a dream. It is truly possible.

Once you have your vision in your mind, you must always remember to follow that dream. Do not give in and decide it does not have merit simply because it is not tangible. As the definition states, "a vision is an anticipation of that which will come," so it is something you see as achievable and something you wish to accomplish. Just do not forget the most important ingredient in achieving it — your team.

Now that you know what your vision is you need to find a way to get your teachers on board to achieve this vision. The easiest way to accomplish this goal is to be passionate about it. Such profound belief is contagious, especially if you are enthusiastic. Notice when your staff does something positive. Any positive step is a step toward achieving your vision, and whoever takes that step, no matter how small, should be applauded.

An exceptional teacher will start the year assessing his or her students. There will be several who have problems, possibly the majority. Nevertheless, to achieve their annual goals, this great teacher will praise and applaud students who take a step, no matter how small or incidental it may seem, because doing so will encourage the other students to do the same. This is an approach teachers have used since the beginning of time, and the same approach will work infect your staff with your vision.

When you have shared your vision with your staff, begin watching for small steps and large strides that will help you achieve your vision everywhere you go. Praise the custodian for searching through the trash to find a student's retainer. During morning announcements thank the drama teacher and the students for putting on such a wonderful performance the night before, then go to the classroom, and thank them in person. Applaud the teacher who consistently rolls out high-achieving students. All these actions on their part are major strides in accomplishing your vision. The acknowledgment on your part will do the same. These types of actions also will influence the belief that your school is making strides in being successful.

Another step in achieving vision is to encourage your teachers and students to experiment. Over the course of the years to come, you will be amazed at how many ideas staff and students will share if you will take the time to listen, and give them the opportunity to experiment. Regardless of the outcome of any experiment the attempt should be applauded. Success is wonderful but so is failure. Trying is the key. If they are not afraid to try something new it means they have faith in you, that it is okay to fail because failing is a learning step, an opportunity to gain knowledge, and a reason to try something new again.

Teachers are swamped every year with newly implemented test ideas in the form of educational research. They become tired and leery of this constant barrage of interference. They are trying, after all, to educate children here, and it tends to make teachers a bit shy of any kind of new ideas; which may well include your vision. Yet there are ways to get around this justified attitude. You should listen when Ms. Stephens slips up during a conversation and makes the statement, "I still say a hands-on approach in

Mr. Smith's oceanography class is the way to go." Be enthusiastic that Ms. Stephens made the suggestion, and then ask her to help you persuade Mr. Smith to try the suggestion. Do not be surprised if Mr. Smith's first reaction is to gawk at you as though you are insane. As previously stated, teachers are tired and suspicious of forced research, and with your enthusiasm, this may be the first thought that enters his mind. Teachers are hesitant to suggest ideas. Their ideas have been shot down so often because of funding, lack of volunteers, liabilities, and scores of other reasons that they ask these questions: Why suggest an idea if you know it will be tossed? Why even exert the energy to think of ideas if they are to be belittled? So when Ms. Stephens looks at you as though you have suddenly sprouted three heads, keep smiling. Keep your enthusiasm bubbling, and again ask for Ms. Stephen's help in convincing Mr. Smith — remain positive.

Once you have convinced Ms. Stephens to join you in talking to Mr. Smith, and she has become infected with your contagious enthusiasm, stay focused on that positive attitude even in the face of problems or negativity. Let us say that Mr. Smith's first reaction is sharing his idea of setting up salt water and fresh water tanks for his students to take care of as part of their grade. Everyone is now getting excited. Mr. Smith suddenly flinches and brings up the lack of funds for this project. Respond to this by taking the project to his classes, and asking the students for suggestions. Assure him that you will help in every way possible: finding volunteers, looking for resources, asking for donations from the community. All of a sudden, what was once merely a dream is now beginning to look possible.

In her book *Gardening in the Minefield: A Survival Guide for School Administrators*, author Laurel Schmidt writes of how she implemented "peer visiting day" to spread her vision. She would teach a class for one period while the assistant principal did the same. This gave two teachers the freedom to observe and ask questions of their peers. She also organized brown bag seminars for lunchtime, giving teachers the opportunity to listen to a guest lecturer while eating lunch.

There are many ways to launch, spread, and propagate the vision for your school, but it is in your best interest to include the parents. Although this is much easier said than done, it is doable. The key is to remember your school parents are diverse. You have supportive parents, involved parents, non-caring parents, and parents who are just waiting for what they perceive as a reason to bash your nonexistent skills. You will find that if you invite the parents to share your vision, and ask for their input, you will win over the majority in due time. You also will gain knowledge, information, friends, volunteers, resources, and possibly some good ideas.

Strong Suit, Weak Hand

Pretend you are playing a card game. You have a number of cards in your hand, and lucky for you, the majority of them are of the same suit. You are excited, certain you are going to win the game, and take home the trophy for best player. You plan to place it on the mantle beside the baseball you caught that was autographed at the last Red Sox win. But wait. The cards are not all the same suit. There seems to be one low card hidden away.

In cards, your strong points may be in one suit, but your hand will be weak unless you are playing a certain game. The same is true when considering your qualities as a leader. Not all your talents are in one area. In this game of cards, the educational game, one strong suit or one strong quality is not enough for you to have landed the job, so we know it is not the case. When assessing and planning strategy for your school, you need a hand with aces and face cards in all suits, just as you, the principal, need strong qualities in many subject areas.

If you only have one teacher who is a quality educator, you are going to fail as a leader. With the variety of subjects a school is responsible for teaching, you need great teachers in many fields. This takes us back to all the necessities for a winning hand; training and tools to make your teachers excellent educators, a supporting staff, a strong community and curriculums that are suited for your students geographic area, a positive relationship with your community, a vision that everyone is willing to work toward, and an unyielding passion for your students' education. All these components combined will give you a royal flush in poker every time. But throw in a three of clubs and your royal flush will go down the drain.

You may wonder where the three of clubs came from. That is what you must discover, and after you find where that three of clubs is hiding, and you force it to show itself, you must decide what to do with it. This is how you begin to put together an important part of your strategy.

We have not gone into detail about the fact that teachers can be detrimental to your career as well as your school. The bottom line is that teachers can make or break your educational institution as well as your vocation.

Getting rid of bad staff is not easy. It can be done but it comes with a cost. Unfortunately, when school administration tries to fire a bad teacher, it can be an endless suction on the district and state money, the teachers' and students' morale, and your sanity. You might not want to take on this battle if there is an easier way.

You want aces and face cards in your hand when you plan the game. The same is true with your teachers. You want the best ones you can possibly get. But what about that three of clubs that was hidden in the mix? What will you do with that?

You must first determine if you have a bad teacher on your hands. Here are some of the telltale signs.

- A good teacher will try to find the problem if all his or her students are doing poorly. A bad teacher will blame everyone else.

- There is a history of phone calls, angry letters, and threats from parents.

- Each day brings students to your office from his or her classroom.

- No amount of training or tools improves the situation or teaching technique.

- Students consistently have bad grades.

- Students do well or average in all their classes with the exception of his or hers.

Once you are certain you are stuck with a bad apple, you must decide what to do with it. This is where you must choose your battles wisely. Although every principal wants a superior teaching staff, few of them have that pleasure. Most principals are happy to have a majority of good teachers, and choose to ignore that one bad apple or three of clubs. Unfortunately, the cost of getting rid of a bad teacher does not outweigh what they hope is only a temporary impact on the students.

A 2002 study in New York found that the average time needed to terminate a teacher is 319 days, and the average cost to complete the termination is $112,000. If the decision is appealed the cost would be almost three times as much. In most states, teachers draw their pay during the dismissal process which means more cost. Most of the time a principal ends up having to sign a letter of recommendation, putting the bad teacher in a good position to find another job. If this is the case, you are simply shoving the problem onto another principal and a slew of other students.

Instead of firing bad teachers, most principals attempt to encourage the teacher to improve, grow, and learn to teach better. This is an impossible task for some, but for others there is usually at least a small amount of improvement. One thing must be noted here, if you do have a bad teacher, you should be sure to keep a log of everything that is said or done.

When you evaluate a bad teacher, you may carefully suggest a different approach or method for him or her to try. This, most likely, will result in a visit from the teacher's union but you should at least try. You could purchase tools, software, or new curriculum, but the truth is it will not make any difference. Any attempt to help a teacher do a better job is necessary, and logging any discussions for improvement, as well as the result of those discussions, is in your best interest.

Thankfully — most principals can say that the majority of their personnel consists of good teachers. There may be some under-performers, but sometimes they can be helped to improve their methods. So how is a principal to overcome the problem of having a three of clubs in an otherwise winning hand? The solution is not always in the firing, but in the hiring. Barbara Belanger, principal of Harbor City Elementary School in Florida, advises first-year principals to "hire teachers who are enthusiastic about kids and have a willingness to learn." John Redd, principal of Bellevue Junior High School in Ohio, advises hiring teachers who "have compassion."

If you are fortunate enough to be able to hire new staff, then do so carefully. Do everything humanly possible to hire worthy teachers, and this will help minimize the few bad teachers you have. You never know — it may even have a positive influence on the bad teachers. Try to avoid a losing and costly battle. Instead of allowing the bad apple to become your focal point, focus on helping your good teachers and hiring good teachers.

According to Principal Barry Pichard, the hiring of teachers is "one of the most important jobs you will do for your school. A great teacher will let you sleep at night, handle parents, get along with students and other staff."

The Strategy, the Overview

Your approach will determine whether your educational institution becomes or continues to be successful . Your approach will either make this happen or make the institution a failure. No pressure here — just fact. It is up to you to be the leader you attended college to become.

As a professor of educational leadership at Indiana State University, Todd Whitaker, did a study involving 163 middle schools. He found three key differences between effective and less effective principals. One significant difference was that the effective principals viewed all aspects of the school as their responsibility. If you want to be a superb principal, this is the first step; you must be willing to accept a huge responsibility.

The second step is your vision. Maintain and feed that vision at every opportunity. Keep a positive attitude, and be sure to applaud those who help make this vision become a reality.

Use your staff wisely and this will come back to you more than tenfold. Your staff is the key to your success just as you are to theirs. The two-way street we previously discussed is most important in achieving your vision and achieving a high-quality institution. Your responsibilities are vast, and it is almost impossible to do everything required. Your staff is the place to find help with those responsibilities. They will help lighten the load, bring information to your door, boost morale, serve as a springboard in the community, soothe the ruffled feathers of parents, teach your students so that they will be successful adults, and carry your vision throughout the remaining years of their career.

Your mentor can help you in many ways, and is an important asset for you; a guide, a helping hand, a sounding board, a place to find suggestions, someone with experience who can help you find peace of mind that you will need more than just once in a while. Let us face it, in your position peace of mind is "gold."

Respect and reflection on the previous leader whose footsteps you follow is a key factor in building relationships with your staff. Do not hurry a mourning process, and do not attempt to make them forget someone they held in high regard. No matter how well organized the previous leader left things, make your own lists and evaluate everything. Be patient and kind, respectful and understanding. In time the previous leader will be remembered fondly for the things he or she did. Your position will become defined soon enough.

Keep your priorities in order. Student education is top priority, but to achieve the best education possible for your students, you must do all that is possible for your staff. If your teachers are teaching the best they know how, then improving their skills is the focus. Teach them new and different methods. Provide tools for them to use in order to improve their teaching skills. Allow them time to visit other classrooms and discuss methods with other teachers. Taking care of your teachers takes care of your students.

Stay out of the office as much as possible. If your main focus is paperwork and phone calls, you will never convince anyone that your top priority is your students' education. Be seen and be heard in order to define your position, and create lasting relationships with your staff. Praise the good work in your school every day, and it will be obvious you are a worthy and caring leader. Treat everyone with respect and expect the same in return. This cannot be stated enough times. Show respect, and you will gain respect. This is a two-way street not only with your staff but with the students, their parents, the community as a whole, your administration, your school board, and anyone else who has a hand in education.

Working with your staff and having them work with you is the key to your strategy. This is how a smooth operation works successfully. With this in mind, we will soon look at whether or not the path from Point A to Point B is leveling out and getting shorter. But first we must discuss a few other necessities.

3
THE STANDARDS

———

There are set standards that school leaders are expected to use as a guideline in their job as principal. Several states have adopted these standards, which were set by the Council of Chief State School Leaders. These guidelines are known as the ISLLC Standards. These profound words were used for restructuring the principal programs at several universities and used as a model to redesign programs for leading principals. The standards state that a principal is a leader who promotes the success of students first and foremost. The wording of the standards leaves no doubt that a principals' top priority is to be the education, health, and safety of the students. The ISLLC Standards can be found in a PDF format online at **www.ccsso.org/content/pdfs/isllcstd.pdf** or the booklet may be purchased for $10.00 by writing to: Council of Chief State School Officers, Attn: Publications, One Massachusetts Avenue NW, Suite 700, Washington, DC 20001-1431.

The values of a principal are for the betterment of his or her students. It is the foundation on which students succeed, teachers reach their learners, and principals become exceptional leaders to help their students contribute to the future of the world. Without these standards, the schools will fail our students who in turn will fail our country. As a principal you are not just a manager of a building with several hundred kids running wild and being scolded by 40 or 50 adults. You are a humane administrator and without the humanity you will be a failure.

There are certain untold rules a great principal will follow when dealing with his personnel and students on a daily basis. First is showing respect for each individual in your building. A quality principal has set standards he or she never waivers from, integrity being the building block on which these values lie. A good principal will never correct one of his or her teachers in the presence of other people. To humiliate another human being in public is to make a loud statement of your idiocy and inhumanity.

A leader with good values will not hesitate to applaud his or her teachers and give them the courtesy of allowing them to have the stage when they are standing on it. A good leader will take every problem that arrives at his or her door with genuine sincerity. A good principal will have a sense of humor and a smile for each person he or she passes. A good principal will respect each individual, from the custodian to the best teacher in the school. Students will be given the chance to redeem themselves after acting inappropriately. A great leader will do all he or she can to understand what caused the student to act inappropriately. To be respected as a principal of worth, he or she will treat students as though the student were his or her own child.

If you look you will find your strength in your school and your community. By being aware of their needs and using all of your talents to achieve your vision for the betterment of your students, the community, the teachers and staff, and the school as a whole, they will support you and give you strength as a leader. As a leader you must be caring. At the same time you must plan to have a well-run environment. You must communicate with the populace of your school. Communication is made easier today with e-mail. But please keep in mind that e-mail can comes across as cold and impersonal. Face-to-face discussions are more personal, appropriate and necessary in order to develop good relationships.

Your job as a school leader is complex, and that is your reality. You have tasks that are innumerable and at times overwhelming, but if you focus on learning, teaching, and school improvement, you will succeed.

Honoring the System

By following the ISLLC standards you will be able to honor the system. The ISLLC standards are moral agents and social advocates for the students and the communities you serve. They are used to value, honor, and care for the individuals in your educational community.

Value, honor, and care are strong words that are imperative for school leaders. Millions of parents put the fate of their children in your hands each day of the week, entrusting you with the care of their most precious possession. This is the main reason it is so important for you, as a leader, to honor the system. As stated in Chapter One there is much more at stake than the mere future of an infinite number of students. Your responsibility spreads from inside the school to beyond the doors of your establishment. Once your students leave your hallowed halls, how they turn out as adults affects your school's community, your state, your country, and most probably, in some way, the whole world. Hopefully they will become adults who are good examples for others. They will teach and educate, and be contributing resources.

The system was set up to educate. To make children valuable resources for the world is truly a burden most would not want to carry. The profession you have chosen is noble and worthy, but it is up to you to ensure the profession is carried out in a noble and worthy way.

With the social fabric of society changing, culture becoming more diverse, poverty increasing, families becoming more complex, and the physical, emotional, mental, and moral welfare of students declining, your job as a school leader is much more multifaceted than it once was. All things that happen in our world can, and usually do, indirectly or directly affect the students in your care. The economic foundations of our society, global economy, technology, market-based solutions, shifting jobs, markets crashing, and the ever-changing world of education are all major contributors to how your community, and the families in your community, are thriving or diminishing. All these contributors will determine how your students are behaving. How you handle those students will have an impact on their lives; in either a good way or a negative way. The pressure is on you, and in order to be a valuable principal you must live up to the standards.

The ISLLC standards are the heart and soul of effective leadership. A school community is a living, breathing entity. As with any living, breathing entity there must be heart and soul for quality of life. For quality of life, children must be educated in a learning environment with high standards. The ISLLC standards have three basics in the framework: knowledge, disposition, and performance. As stated by the Council of Chief State School Officers, "As we became more enmeshed in the work, we discovered that dispositions often occupied center stage."

A principal's disposition affects the whole working environment of a school. If you are in a foul mood, it will affect everyone around you, everyone those people are around, and so on. Your disposition will determine how the day will be for hundreds of people, not just one or two. Your disposition on learning, on being productive, on vision, on respect works together; all of it rests on your shoulders. You have freedom over your actions, and it is up to you to maintain a good disposition. Your good humor and caring will spread from one person to another creating an environment that will enhance learning. Like your vision a good disposition is contagious.

Whether it is acknowledged the principal is the center of the action within the school. Everyone goes to the principal with a problem that involves another person of the school community or the education of the school community: a teacher, a student, a staff member, a parent, the cook, the custodian, the PTO or PTA president, a school board member, the mayor, the media, even the city council. All things revolve around you. You are the one who will leave the lasting impression. That impression will be based on your disposition, knowledge, and skills. How you react to a situation or request, discuss the situation or request, realize the situation or request, discover a solution, implement the solution, take action, and follow up with your action will determine your relationship with the community and your reputation as a leader. You and you alone will set the tone for the whole school community. It is up to you to not only make the tone enthusiastic, genuine, and positive, but also to present an example of such.

What you prepared for in college was sufficient for setting goals, implementing curriculums and programs, observing classroom teaching methods, understanding law and legislature, mandating and dispersing monies, coordinating auxiliary support systems, hiring, firing, promoting and dismissing, providing resources, preparing for standardized tests and achievements, and organizing school activities and events. These things are where your skills and knowledge are required. There are areas where skills and knowledge are not enough.

What the colleges and universities cannot prepare you for are the small and large daily tasks. You will deal with disputes, arguments, fights, leaking water pipes, broken water fountains, a faulty boiler, a wrecked bus, and a crying student whose parents are in the middle of a bitter divorce. Sometimes there are disasters, adversities, and tragedies, during which you are expected to maintain leadership and remain control. Along with the negative, daily incidents you also must deal with accomplishments, phone calls of approval, slaps on the back, and a multitude of other requests. There will be community events to attend, blessings of good fortune to acknowledge, and success of staff and students that will need to be remembered and mentioned. The harmless but distracting class clown will become your problem, the food fights your dilemma, and the broken copier that chewed up the state letter on new programs is in your hands. The marine biology teacher's leaking aquarium that short-circuited the electrical plug is up to you to have repaired, and sometimes theatrics will find their way to your office. All these incidents and more require your good disposition, your heart, and soul.

In order to deal with everything that comes to your desk, you must be able to maintain a sense of humor when necessary, but also know when a good sense of humor is appropriate. You must be able to feel a parent or student's sense of loss, regret, or redemption. You must be able to keep control, be patience and remember that the people you are dealing with might be having a bad day too. In most situations, it is not necessarily the solution that matters most, but how you deal with the problems at hand. You need tact, integrity, sincerity, and a good relationship with your school community to have a functioning open door policy.

Your personal values and standards will determine your values and standards as a principal. If you consider your school community your second family, you will succeed in becoming a leader who will produce quality teachers and resourceful students; students who will become contributing adults.

A principal must, however, remember that he or she cannot be "all things to all people." Trying to please everyone can cause more conflicts than not. It is important to do what you feel is right for the student or the school community as a whole, and not always what the person sitting on the other side of your desk wants you to do. In order to do the best by your school community you must look at each situation, consider your professional standards, and genuinely see the situation as a problem for whomever brought it to your door. Follow up by applying your skills, intelligence, and disposition to the situation, and then pray.

Two things can help you define and produce results for all situations: your vision and your standards. What is best for the student? What is best for the education of the student? What is best for the school community as a whole? Sometimes a situation will conflict with the answers to these questions. You must judge if what is best for the student is best for the school community as a whole. If some of the problems in your school involve a violent and threatening situation, it is obvious that you, as leader, must ask yourself what is best for the school community rather than what is best for the student. These decisions are not always easy, but you must remember you are doing the best that you can for your second family; as a family, there is nothing more they can ask of you. Be consistent and reliable, and base your actions on your standards and vision. You will be showing the school community that you are sticking to priorities; that you are a valuable leader. This type of leader sleeps much better at night than others do.

In all situations a principal must be diplomatic. You may not say what the person sitting across the desk wants to hear, but if you say it right, they will be grateful for your taking the time to listen to them, and most likely leave the office with respect for your position. There will be times when it will not matter what you say or how you say it. But those times will be few if you strive for diplomacy, and show you are capable of becoming a great leader with high standards. Showing genuine sincerity and concern will get you much further than if you take an attitude of "I am the leader, and I have the last say." You will fail miserably with such an attitude and your reputation will be tarnished — possibly forever.

Education and the schools that provide it are under constant scrutiny and attack in today's society. With new technology, word of mouth spreads much farther and faster than ever before. Sometimes it causes embarrassment and uncalled-for judgments. The world is much more complex today which means the world of education is much more complex. With fast changes, fast-paced news, fast social reforms, and fast technology, the true story is many times distorted and exaggerated before it becomes a headline. In order to deal with such injustices or embarrassments a principal must be able to stay focused, be honest, abide by his standards, and remember to keep the best interest of his or her school community as top priority. A principal will have to be open to criticism, wrongful judgments, and unnecessary public humiliation, but will still sleep better at night if the school community is his or her top priority.

In researching this book, it became apparent that there are other major changes in the world of education — the overwhelming public concern for the cost of education, and the public outcry for accountability. In Laurel Schmidt's book, *Gardening in the Minefield: a Survival Guide for School Administrators*, she points out that it is not just your community that is watching. As a principal you are being watched by many more eyes than usual: state and federal legislators, special interest groups, taxpayers, the media, private enterprises, big businesses, the local business community, the board of education, your superintendent, the parents, school site governance groups, the teacher's union, and the teachers themselves.

With constant monitoring and inspection from public and private sectors, it seems necessary to remind you of the importance of being a good leader. Only a leader with vision, a leader with standards, and a leader whose top priority is the students' right to a quality education will pass public and private scrutiny. Not only will you sleep better at night but your school will thrive, your teachers will be your team in educating the students, and your school community will be your support in times of turmoil and tribulation. One day your school will fall under the media's microscope and if you are a good principal, your school community as a whole will pass inspection and the intense search for fault will come to a screeching halt. Good leaders know how to deal with issues that are challenging and uncalled for, and good leaders will keep their school community standing on solid ground long after an unjustified search for blame ends.

4
LAW AND LITIGATION

———

You probably know that control and funding for education in America comes from three sources: federal government, state government, and local government. Students have the option of public school, private school, or home school. In public and private schools education is divided into three levels: elementary, junior high or middle school, and high school. The progress is simple; divide the students by age groups, place them in the school of their parent's choice, and give them a quality education. Simple, right? I am sure you are thinking, "Oh my, if only it were that simple."

With more than 76.6 million students enrolled in schools across America, and more than 5,000 employees working for the United States Department of Education, it is a blessing the federal government is not heavily involved in determining the curriculums or educational standards in our schools. But things have changed slightly since the No Child Left Behind Act, which was signed into law by President George W. Bush on March 23, 2007.

It has been stated that our country has a reading literacy rate of 98 percent with the population over the age of 15, but many teachers, principals, and professors might argue that statement.

In America school begins at the age of five or six. To graduate from high school a student will complete 13 years of education. One would think all students graduating from high school would have the ability to read and write at the same level; that of a young adult. This, unfortunately, is not always the case.

Where are the schools failing the students? Why are the schools failing the students? Is it really the schools that are failing, or is it the families?

Placing blame is not our focus, but at the same time, one would have to be daft not to realize it is a major concern that weighs heavily on all principals; new and veteran alike.

Review some of the goals set for principals by local, state, and federal departments.

It is understood that curricular decisions vary in school systems along with teaching and learning techniques. Individual school systems determine public education curriculums based on a state's learning standards. Adequate Yearly Progress (AYP) must meet the goals set by state and school districts, but now the AYP is mandated by the No Child Left Behind Act. Today a typical classroom will include children with special needs which adds to the responsibilities of the teachers and the principals, as do the demands of the Individuals with Disabilities Act (IDEA), which also must be met. State learning standards have been around for a number of years but now the federal laws of No Child Left Behind mandates standards at state levels.

The IDEA is federal law passed in 2004. It requires each state to provide services that meet the individual needs of students with special needs. The IDEA also requires that students be placed in the Least Restrictive Environment (LRE). The Least Restrictive Environment requirement means you must meet with parents to create an Individualized Education Program. This will determine where each child is best placed for his or her education. If the school fails to place a student appropriately, the parents can take the school district to court.

Under the No Child Left Behind Act all states must test students in public schools. This is to ensure they are getting the minimum level of education they are guaranteed. Along with this mandate it is required that students and schools show Adequate Yearly Progress.

Standardized testing was based on China's imperial examinations which covered the Six Arts during the Han dynasty. The Six Arts included knowledge of rituals and ceremonies, music, archery, math, and writing.

The world's largest private educational testing and measurement organization, the Educational Testing Service, was established in 1948, and operates with an annual budget of $900 million. In 1965 the Elementary and Secondary Education Act required standardized testing in public schools. The No Child Left Behind Act of 2001 tied the knot of public funding to standardized testing.

An advantage of standardized testing is that the results can be documented and scores can be shown. This is an advantage for admissions in higher education when trying to compare students from across the nation or the world. There is a disadvantage to standardized testing; school district leaders want funding and are tempted to have principals place test curriculum in the classroom, i.e., teachers are essentially teaching for the tests. Test preparation is a growing concern, and is another factor in the stress level of students which is drastically rising. The stress level of students has recently become such an issue that many schools are implementing activities such as yoga that are stress reducers.

None of the facts you just read were new to you. The fact that the responsibilities just keep growing and the weight more burdening is something you were aware of when you made the decision to become a principal. While you were attending college you were taught that whether or not a school operates effectively would determine the chances of a student's academic success. This leads us to examine your involvement in curriculums, instruction, and assessment.

To date your involvement is considered critical by many. Some believe your knowledge of subject matter is as important as the teachers'. In a study on leadership by researchers at the National Institute on Educational Governance, your willingness to provide input on classroom practices is highly valued by teachers. Most teachers would welcome regular meetings with the principal to obtain assessment of practices and instructional feedback. The only way this can truly be beneficial to teachers is if you are knowledgeable in their domains. Let us face it — it can be beneficial if you know your stuff. This works because it is how you can best give guidance.

In order to meet federal, state, and local district standards, and give the best guidance possible to your teachers, it is highly advisable for principals to have regular meetings with other administrators. This is the best way to stay aware of current changes and advances in curriculums.

Some curriculums are guaranteed, and some are simply practical. When a curriculum is guaranteed, a school is responsible for determining that classroom teachers teach specific content, in specific classes, for specific grade levels. There have been many heated arguments over why the same basic curriculums, such as math, writing, reading, and science, are not taught in each school across the nation. But the truth is that if every school used the same curriculums, it still would not be taught by the same methods. You can give every teacher the same book, and require they teach the same content, but each teacher is an individual, and will use different methods to teach. They may add to, or even leave out portions of content. There is just no feasible way to know what students have been taught. There is another problem with standardized testing; if certain content of a curriculum is mandated, how is it monitored? If each teacher teaches differently, how does standardized testing really work? Does it show that students are being taught their guaranteed curriculums? As a leader, it is up to you to make sure standardize testing is done properly.

The Risk Factor

To add insult to injury it seems that every time a new mandate is handed down it is later improved, changed, added to, or more mandates are piled on top of the previous ones. When the Columbine disaster took place in 1999, student safety became a hot issue. Suddenly the public had concerns about their children's safety. State departments began screaming about making the schools a safer environment. Local districts passed the panic on to the administrators, and principals everywhere had a new issue to acknowledge, and a solution to find and implement within a certain time period. What few people seem to consider is the fact that in another four or five years the disaster plans will not matter. There will be something new, and possibly horrible which will take place, and all the money spent on the disaster plans will be wasted. The truth is that there is no way to cover all the possible scenarios. A good analogy is a computer virus. Every time a new virus is used to infect computers across the world, another computer whiz will develop a new patch to contain and destroy the virus. Then another computer geek creates a different and more intense virus, and the beat goes on.

As noted mandated tests are constantly changing, evolving, and becoming more intense and demanding. The best leaders have shown that if they ignore the panic button about standardized testing and screaming department heads insisting they bring test scores up, and simply continue to assure that their students have the best education they can possibly give them, the test scores fall into place naturally. The most effective principals have stated they think of standardized testing as a means for improving curriculums.

Every decision you make as a principal should fall back on what is best for your students. As a principal it is up to you to stay abreast of what is being learned by your students. To provide the best instructional leadership you must work with your teachers and create committees, then in turn, work with your committees to consistently assess the curriculums. By working with your staff on the curriculums, you will hold discussions that will lead to new ideas and improvement in teaching and in student achievement. It also is up to you to inform your committees and your teachers, of any new state mandates. Regular meetings provide you the time needed to pass this information on to them, implement new curriculums, and guide them in new approaches.

It is also up to you to consistently assess and renew curriculums, and determine whether it is working for your students, as well as your teachers. As we have already stated, the success of the students is the determining factor in whether the curriculum is working. The time dedicated to curriculum development is essential to being a quality leader.

In small districts, it usually is up to the principal to be a significant player in developing curriculums. In larger districts, a principal usually sits on a curriculum committee and is expected to scrutinize stated curriculums, assure it is being taught, and verify it is working in student progress. Curriculums, or the written plans for what students should know, includes knowing about the student and the social surroundings of the school. Placing the correct curriculum in the correct community is essential. Curriculum also includes content and concepts that students will, or will not, come across in life situations. This is a factor in deciding which curriculum is best for your students.

Standardized tests are supposed to be used to assess student achievement in certain curriculum areas. This is why great principals see standardized testing as a means to help them in their quest for better curriculums. By discussing standardized testing with your teachers within this concept, it will lessen the burden and worry of student scores.

Along with the constant assessing for instructional leadership, state and federal mandates, as well as district mandates, you must also be sure to follow stated mandates for special needs students. These mandates can include special education, remedial assistance, adding programs for special gifts and talents, English as a second language, and related services for children with disabilities. All students are entitled to the best education possible, and these special needs must be met. There are legal requirements principals must implement for these federal and state mandates, and if they are not met, there are legal consequences. You must know the laws regarding these mandates and be sure all procedures are followed.

In the Individuals with Disabilities Education Act, the federal law governs how state and public agencies are to provide for these children from birth to the age of 21. It is considered a civil rights law, and school districts can be sued if they fail to follow all procedures. Funds are readily available to states that comply with the minimum policies and procedures regarding the education for children with disabilities. These mandates were put into place to guarantee a free, appropriate public education that will prepare children with disabilities for employment and independent living.

A student does not automatically qualify for special education services just because they have a disability. Under the IDEA, a student who does qualify is defined as a child with mental retardation, hearing impairments, speech impairments, language impairments, visual impairments, serious emotional disturbance, orthopedic impairments, autism, traumatic brain injury, specific learning disabilities, and other health impairments. These children are protected by Section 304 of the Rehabilitation Act of 1973. Students who do not qualify may fall under accommodations or modifications under the Americans with Disabilities Act (ADA).

Discipline of a child with disabilities is another concern and has terms that must be followed. It is stated under IDEA laws that the disability of a student must be taken into account before disciplining said student. If a child with autism rushes out of the room where there are consistently loud noises and activity, the child's sensitivity to loud noise and excessive activity must be taken into account. This same concept holds true for all students with disabilities according to the laws.

The United States Department of Education states that a child with a disability who has been suspended for ten days total for each school year must have a demonstration purpose, or a "manifestation determination" hearing, within ten school days. This hearing will take place before any decision on the placement of that student can be reached. The hearing will determine if the student's conduct in question was:

- Caused by or had a direct relationship to the child's disability, or was...

- The direct result of the local education agency failed attempt to implement the Individualized Education Program.

If it is determined that the conduct was due to the child's disability, the Individualized Education Program team then must:

- Implement a behavioral intervention plan

- Review the behavioral intervention plan, and modify as necessary

- Return the student to the placement from which he or she was removed.

Safeguards are designed to protect the rights of children with disabilities as well as those of their families. These safeguards were placed to ensure that children with disabilities received a free, appropriate public education.

The amount of time, effort, energy, and paperwork that goes into making sure the Individuals with Disabilities Education Act, Americans with Disabilities Act, and the Individualized Education Program are followed is massive. These restrictions and regulations alone take tons of paperwork, which in turn means time. This is one of many criticisms of the Individuals

Disabilities Education Act. School personnel also worry that although the Individual Disabilities Education Act protects students with disabilities and their families, it does not protect districts, schools or teachers. With being pressed to accomplish so many tasks already, and with having so many requirements to meet for special needs students, there is a lot of pressure. Pressure leads to stress, and sometimes stress leads to mistakes or oversights. This leads to the possibility of a parent getting upset and deciding the laws are not being met for their child. They can take you to court, but this is only a fraction of the problem.

The fact that there was an oversight could have been caused by funding. While the government made restrictions that were to be followed, it promised funding to help ensure these restrictions could be met. The government promised to supply 40 percent of the cost to the districts in educating students with disabilities. As of 2007 the government had paid for approximately 12 percent of the costs in supplying needs and education for students with disabilities. If a child who attends your school is in a wheelchair you must have wheelchair accessible ramps. These ramps are expensive and the money must come from somewhere. Regardless of where the money comes from, by law, it must be done.

More pressure. More stress. More responsibilities.

This leads us to other criticisms of the Individualized Disabilities Education Act that should be mentioned. Some parents blame the schools for not designing and implementing plans that are required by the law. Some parents think there should be consistent monitoring of these laws to ensure they are being put into place. Some parents and families also believe the overseer of the hearings on the requirements is not impartial. It has also been stated by some parents that the government allows districts to spend more money fighting parents who want special services for their disabled children, than money that would be spent placing these services. Many parents worry that schools will react against families or the child when demands are made for the child.

Then there is the worry over the outcry that children are labeled "learning disabled" when they are not disabled. There have been accusations that minorities have been placed as students with learning disabilities more than they should be. And last but not least, parents are worried about not having the knowledge to prepare an Individualized Education Program form, causing them to worry about schools inadequately preparing them.

Pressure, stress, and responsibilities are never ending for a principal. Moreover, this is only a portion of your worries. Also, there is the fact that politics are dipping into the fray.

Politics in Education

You are being watched by many people. Schools, teachers, principals, superintendents, school districts, and state and federal government are constantly criticizing schools when it comes to education. Even though it seems to be a regression of our society, schools are where the blame is often placed.

I currently work two jobs. At one, I am a supervisor. The second job is my writing business. I speak to many people on many levels, and I have heard numerous complaints about how hard it is to find competent people to work. Another constant grievance is trying to communicate with someone who knows what they are doing when dealing with, or putting forth, complaints in the business world. As a businessperson and a supervisor, I admit I have experienced both scenarios.

I have witnessed, many times over, the problem with hiring new employees. The majority of the people who apply for a job cannot pass the drug test. If they manage to get past the drug screening, they cannot handle the hand-eye coordination test. If they manage to pass the drug test and the hand-eye coordination tests, they bomb the written test. Most applications are full of misspellings, and this can sometimes include their own name and address. It is a sad state of affairs, but it is the truth.

Where does the fault of these facts lie? Who has failed these adults that they cannot read, write, or function as an adult?

Due to the problems of a regressing society, people are looking for somewhere to place blame and the schools seem to be the main target. What the industries, politicians, business owners and human resource personnel are not realizing is one simple solution: it is their responsibility to hire productive individuals. Schools churn out millions of students every year, and these students are then considered adults. Some of them will read and write with above average abilities. Some of them will read and write at a fourth-grade level. Did some of the schools fail these students? Probably. Did their parents failed them? Yes they did. Is it the fault of the school that a business owner hires an incapable employee? No, it is not.

It all comes down to taking the share of responsibility and accepting that responsibility. At the same time, the principal in School B should not be blamed for the failure of being an effective leader by the principal in School A. As with any entity, there are good leaders and bad leaders, but somehow our society has managed to lump all schools into one big, ugly group.

A good place to start in assessing students entering the adult world is looking within one's self. As parents, teachers, principals, business owners, managers, and supervisors, each person can make a difference. The learning experience does not end after high school graduation. In many ways, it just begins. Each person who touches the life of a child is the inconsistent entity, or the consistent entity, in the life of that child and that same life as an adult. Each person can make a difference if they take this fact to heart. Many good leaders have stated it is imperative that they accept their responsibility to guarantee not only the best education possible for their students, but also to be a positive influence on those students.

So what is a principal to do when they hear it is their fault that a student entering the adult world cannot read and write? If you are doing your job as you know it should be done, you are to keep this comforting fact close to your heart and sleep well at night.

We know education is now in a perpetual state of reform. Your role as principal has changed dramatically. Schools are made up of multifaceted communities. You have groups of outsiders who will make decisions for your schools on everything from which textbooks your teachers will use to what your budget will be. While you are busy doing all the things we have already discussed, you must please these outsiders with your students standardized tests scores jumping through the roof as though each of them walked past you in single file to stick their finger in an electrical plug.

Meanwhile you must deal with the eyes that are watching and the devils that are riding your heels like the hounds of hell. Principal of Bellevue Junior High School in Ohio, John Redd, stated the obvious quite eloquently: "Politicians want to be the watchdogs of education; they just do not want to take the blame when the proper funding is not there."

There are many people watching and observing the outcome of your students with keen interest. The list is a bit intimidating but it is a list well worth observing and thinking about. As Laurel Schmidt states in her book, *Gardening in the Minefield*, "while you may have only the vaguest notion," these watchers exist, and it is best to know they are there and why.

Education today is a multi-trillion dollar enterprise, and to survive it you need to know who the political people are and why they are so interested in what you are doing. The truth is that education today attracts big business and big power because of the money involved and because of the current public demands. The following list of people who are interested in your educational institution was devised by Laurel Schmidt:

- State and federal legislatures

- Taxpayers

- Special interest groups

- The media

- Private enterprise

- Big business

- Local business community

- Parents

- Board of education

- Teachers' union

- Your superintendent

- Teachers.

- School site governance groups

> *Schools are sometimes the scapegoat of our society."*
>
> **Barry Pichard, Principal**
> Sunrise Elementary School
> Palm Bay, Florida

Many groups benefit politically when you fail to succeed in having student achievement in your building. Let us take a look at these watchers, and discuss how they benefit from what they consider to be your failure.

State and Federal Legislatures

Politicians are always looking for something to use to their benefit. They want to claim they can meet the demands of our society, and they do make this claim, especially during an election year. Before campaigning they are going to take notice of what the concerns of their constituents are, and they are going to pounce like a lion on its prey. While campaigning they are going to assure the people they have a solution to these concerns, and they will implement said solutions as soon as they are voted into office. Sounds all too familiar, does it not? The sad truth is these politicians do get voted into office. They then take their rhetoric which is based on few facts with almost no input from educators, and make new laws that the schools and you as principal must abide by. This means that you must follow the law to a "T," even if you know it is not in the school's best interest.

Special Interest Groups

These groups of people find a criticism and use it to empower their assembly. They lobby the politicians, donate large amounts of money, finance people who run for the school boards, and cause more problems than they solve. These groups pressure politicians and school board candidates to do something, anything, about students with disabilities, cultural problems in communities, racial issues, school vouchers, sex education, health education, obese students, anorexic students, gender issues, and much more.

Taxpayers

Even those who have no children in school must pay taxes that are used to support the schools. This is true for most cities, towns, villages, and communities. Due to the drain on their money, they want to know, and have every right to know, where their money is being spent. Rather than attend school board meetings to learn this information firsthand, they sometimes listen to their neighbors or read criticisms in the newspaper.

I would like to make a note at this point. I have personally witnessed a superintendent that made it mandatory for principals in his district to churn out letters in favor of passing a school levy. The superintendent also demanded that the teachers give a daily speech on the necessity of the same when a school levy was up for voting. There are pros and cons in doing something of this nature. Although the letters were mostly accepted as predictable and somewhat understandable, there were those who argued it was another proven point of how money in schools is wasted. However, the teachers giving a speech had the most adverse affect; parents became irate when their children were used for sending home a political message.

The Media

Newspapers and the television media love to report bad news. School shootings, sexual molestation by teachers, low test scores, negative school board campaigns, and anything else that can cause readers to purchase a paper will be reported. Seldom is a school listed in the newspaper as being an institution that has surpassed tests scores or had high numbers of students graduate with honors. The media has a huge influence on how communities see their schools and even how the public across the nation judge our schools. When a teacher or a coach has sex with a 17-year-old student, it becomes national news. When a school has so many students making the honor roll four years in a row that it cannot pick a valedictorian, the story might make the local paper's Letters to the Editor column. Never forget and always be prepared — the media is always watching for a story.

Private Enterprise

This is where school-based management has become a lucrative target for new commercial enterprises. These enterprises move in when schools are failing and decentralize control from district offices. The control is then taken by an organization such as Edison Schools Inc., a group that partners with school districts to create innovative programs that help students reach their potential. When schools fail in student achievement these private enterprises are reported, especially by the media, as a solution to the problem. Now it is stated by many that there is not enough evidence to evaluate the outcome.

Big Business

There are businesses that publish and distribute standardized tests, textbooks for curriculum, data-processing services, and test preparation materials such as study books for SATs and ACTs. Failing schools are good for these businesses. If a school is not putting out achieving students, they will try new curriculums that require new textbooks. If students are not doing well on standardized tests, these businesses will publicize their materials to have schools purchase said materials, claiming they will help students achieve higher scores.

Local Business Community

Schools with higher achieving students are assets for local business. In being able to claim having one of the best schools in the region, the chamber of commerce, Rotary, real estate agents, and city councils have an easier time bringing in new business, selling homes, and new acquiring new members of the community, which will then pay city taxes. The business community likes to see local schools with successful students due to their stake in education. Not only does it bring in new candidates for hiring, but schools that have excellent students also bring about candidates for future employment.

The Board of Education

School board members have an interest in successful students for various reasons. Many board members will remain citizens of the community and work for the school board as long as they are reelected. Their interest comes from a personal investment, and the aversion to e-mail and phone calls from irate parents. The school board also has the worry of bad media, just as you do, and wants to avoid the stress just as much. There are school board members who want to start their political career at the school board level, and then move up in the ranks after serving. Their interest is understood without further ado.

The Superintendent

The average time for a superintendent to stay with one school district is a bit more than three years. Some superintendents will move on when a majority of new school board members are voted in or there has become a conflict of beliefs in how the school should be run. It is not uncommon for a superintendent to resign or be fired in the middle of his or her contract. This sometimes leads to payment without service adding to the drain on the school districts budget.

Parents

The opinions of the parents matter to a good leader. A principal realizes the value of the parents' judgment of how the school is run. Parents can make or break, not only the job of the principal, but the reelection of a school board, and the money that is given to the school. There are parents who keep a constant watch on the schools, and these parents usually have an open door policy understanding with the superintendent. This can be bad or good, depending on your superintendent, as there will be times the parents will go straight to him instead of speaking with the person in question first and following the chain of command.

School Site Governance Groups

These are school-based management groups that usually consist of administrators, principals, teachers, parents, and other community members holding control of decisions at each school site. They have control of the budget, school improvements, and sometimes have subcommittees that find new curriculums and the hiring of new staff, then get their approval to implement such. There are pros and cons to such groups and the fact that principals must work so closely with what can be diverse conflicts can be challenging to say the least.

Teachers' Unions

Unions are a good thing for some situations and a horrible headache for others. Although they do a good job in representing the teachers, they also hinder the firing of personnel that can ruin what would otherwise be a safe and or learning environment for students. A principal cannot evaluate a teacher as he or she sees fit without interruption from the union. There are also concerns about teachers who are alleged molesters having the freedom to move from one state to another, and sometimes in-state from one school district to another, without the records of the teacher being readily available.

Teachers

These are the people who can ensure educational success for the students of your school, and yet, they are usually the last people to know of reform taking place in the schools. Due to their aversion to politics, they normally refrain from being involved in such matters unless it is due to self-preservation.

Although these people are watching you and your school's progress, or lack thereof, it must be said that most parents are satisfied with the education their children are receiving. Just another good thought to keep close to your heart while you sleep at night.

Michael I. Rothfeld, lecturer and political consultant, said, "The media in the U.S. is overwhelmingly committed to big government, gun control, and the supremacy of state-controlled education over parent-controlled education." This is an issue with many parents, simply because government officials usually have no idea about how education is run; how curriculum is assessed, chosen and implemented; or how the schools really work. Sadly the same is true for many parents. Maybe if we had more politicians such as former North Carolina Governor James Hunt, the politicians would know the workings of education and could make some sound decisions before passing laws that do not work.

Former Governor Hunt was known to speak on the heroics of good educational leaders and the importance of a good education during his four terms. Now he is holding true to his claims of having tremendous admiration for such with the Hunt Institute. The Hunt Institute was established in 2001, and is a nonprofit agency affiliated with the 16 campuses of the University of North Carolina. Hunt is leading the way in educating governors, state leaders, and other political, business, and educational leaders in education policy. The Institute was created for advising ways to implement strategies, and make legal changes to improve educational programs. North Carolina public schools, according to the Rand Corporation, are reported to have improved test scores more than any other state in the 1990s.

With so many eyes watching your progress or failure, you are sure to feel the pain of such scrutiny at some time in your career. This is a sad fact. Just do your job and try to stay aware of the political ranting, and claims going on in your district and state as well as on a federal level. More importantly remember there are parents and students who respect what you do every day. They understand the complexities of your job, the burdens you must carry and the small cheers you seldom hear for your accomplishments.

5
RESPONSIBILITIES

The responsibilities keep coming and there seems to be no end in sight. In a recent conversation regarding the principal's tasks, Gary Brown, principal of Collier School, said it perfectly, "There are not enough hours in a day." This statement is true as you know, but there is more we must discuss.

The role of leader comes with many burdens. Student success is just one, albeit a most important one, and it requires much hard work to attain. Also the assessment and implementation of curriculums call for a diplomatic approach. You must assure the development of teachers and be consistent in finding resources for your them. These are but a few of the principal's responsibilities that we have discussed and yet there are many more.

It is best to implement new curriculums slowly; but we need to be more precise and explain "why" more thoroughly. The explanation will help you when trying to implement change.

Also, conflict with teachers bears mentioning; this is minimal in most schools, but it does occur. This is a crucial part of the job, and you must be prepared to deal with the consequences or the damage could become irreparable; as detailed more thoroughly later in this chapter.

The best way to do a good job is to be prepared, and preparing for your role as a leader is something this book can only help you with. For the most part, it is up to you. We are here to do all we can to make your career choice easier. After all the future of our students is in your hands, and the students are our future. It is in our best interest to help you be a quality leader.

> *As a public school administrator, there is no room for designer heels.*
>
> **"Principal, Pamela Mitchell**
> Central Middle School, Florida

Communication

The principal is viewed as an authority figure. Once you become the principal you may find that some teachers will not be as forthcoming in their communication. In their eyes you are not one of the them but one of the administrative figures. This view may cause some first-year principals to step back and reconsider their approach; which is advisable. How do you maintain open lines of communication without endangering your leadership role? The answer is to be respectful of others at all times. Think about how you would prefer an authority figure to approach you, then communicate with your teachers in the same fashion.

If you make work a pleasant experience rather than a dreaded chore, teachers will love you. If you create an atmosphere that is pleasant to work in, teachers will be inclined to love working for you. If you give recognition when it is deserved, your staff will follow you anywhere you go. Praise your teachers for the outstanding work they do, and your gift will be given back tenfold. If you praise your staff in front of an audience, that is even better. If you commend a teacher with each newsletter you send to parents, you will boost morale and create a buzz throughout the community.

By commending your teachers in various forms, you are communicating your vision and inviting the teachers to become part of your team. You are grooming your relationships with your personnel and this is the path to having a successful team.

There are many obstacles for a first-year principal, but they can all be overcome. All things are possible if you keep the lines of communication strong and positive.

As with all organizations, the success of a school depends on communication and information. Information is essential and there are many ways to communicate. Keeping teachers, staff and personnel on the same page is your job. Although nothing substitutes for personal contact, here are few ways to communicate: memos, meetings, e-mail, committees, and bulletin boards. Face-to-face meetings, however, are essential in building relationships and trust. One-on-one conversations are a good way to let your teachers know you are not there to tell them how to do their job, but to help them do their job to the best of their ability. Never forget that informed teachers are happy teachers.

Sometimes you will find yourself in the position of listening to the personal problems of your staff. It is inevitable that there will be occasions when personal problems will affect the work of your teachers. When they come to you it is because they have integrity, they have a leader they trust, and they are looking for guidance or a good listener. In being a caring leader you will listen out of concern for your staff and your school. If possible, it is up to you to help the teacher find a smooth path to a solution that will not hinder his or her job. There may be incidents that suggest the teacher seek professional help, but do not be surprised if this suggestion is met with resistance. Each incident will be different, but it is up to you to help at least to the point of not allowing the problem to affect the person's work.

It is important to mention that you cannot, and should not, take on the personal problems of your staff. There is a fine line between listening as a leader, and listening to gripes and complaints that do not concern the job of staff members. If you are not careful, you will have every staff member at your school coming to you with every personal problem they have. This is not a good place to be; it will take time, energy, and repair when you have to draw the line later.

In our fast-paced society technology is constantly changing, but this is a good place to start when searching for ideas to suggest change. You will need to encourage teachers to attend seminars, classes, or training for personal growth and professional development. To approach the issue you may want to find a way to make the idea of a seminar inviting, rather than a suggestion that is met with groaning despair. You could try to find humor in the situation or perhaps give them a good reason to look forward to taking part in learning something new. Not only is it important your teachers get consistent opportunities for professional development, it is a formula for disaster if they do not. Education is like a pool of water. If the water stays still, and has no movement or fresh water added, it becomes stagnant. Education is the same. If teachers do not have personal growth and professional development, they become stagnant and cannot do a good job; it means the teachers will not succeed and students will not flourish.

Vision and teamwork are the two elements that should take place in your school every day. A good way to get new teachers on board, working with these two elements, is to create a committee of veteran teachers to guide them. By doing so you are recognizing the skills of your veteran teachers, and simultaneously, welcoming new teachers into the fold.

Speaking of new teachers — you may want to consider protecting them against those teachers who are always negative. You always hope not to have negative teachers, but chances are you will have at least one, maybe more. Survival can become a top priority for a new teacher if they are left on their own. It is not only in your school's best interest to have a mentor for new teachers, it is in your best interest as well. This approach will help prevent possible negativity from the new teachers in the future while assuring they will become part of the team.

Teachers and principals alike dread the boring and sometimes patronizing staff meetings; seldom do teachers gain anything of value from them. Rather than recognize the teachers' work or ask for their priceless input these meetings are dry, dull and meaningless. This problem is being brought to your attention because you are the principal. You can change this dreaded experience and make it a practice your teachers look forward to. Ask your teachers for their opinion on staff meetings and you might be surprised by the negativity. Ask for their suggestions on how to make the meetings an asset and you might get some feedback. For your first staff meeting, develop a plan that will motivate them and boost their morale, and you will find a room full of passionate and creative adults.

The teachers are the people who develop projects for their students. They put ideas into motion, and they can do the same for one another. Put the meetings into the hands of your teachers, and ask them to pick a goal and develop ideas to achieve the goal; you will find your load as a leader has become considerably lighter.

Communication is important just as the play of words is powerful. Always choose your wording carefully, because if you do not, what you present to your staff can be interpreted in a way that is totally erroneous. When you first explain your expectations to your teachers, you must do so diplomatically, but also clearly. You do not want teachers walking out of your first meeting with the impression that your expectations are merely suggestions.

There are so many ways to communicate with people today that it can be overwhelming. There are faxes, e-mail and voice-mail messages; direct lines of communication with letters, school and district mail delivery, cell phone messages, and instant messaging. These are all forms of contact that you cannot afford to ignore. To top it off, you must acknowledge any subpoenas, handwritten notes, post-it notes, phone calls, beepers, walkie-talkies, and face-to-face meetings. With all these forms of communication, you might wonder how on earth you will find the time to walk the halls to observe and build relationships with your students and teachers.

The best way to deal with all these forms of communication is to pick a day to answer them, unless of course, it is an emergency. Another means of dealing with all the communication is to limit what is public. Your e-mail address can be private but that is a matter of choice. You can silence your voice mail and only answer it at the end of the day; restrict phone calls to certain school hours. Instant messaging probably should be private, and phone messages can be handled in priority form set by your secretary after you explain how you wish this to be done. As long as your time is spent with the students' best interest as first priority, there are few who will find fault in the decision to limit the forms of communication. It needs to be noted that even if you limit the calls you take, you are going to be swamped with messages. These calls should be logged by your secretary in a way you find easy and efficient to review and answer accordingly.

As a principal you will find that making your way down the hall to the library will become close to impossible. Although you have good intentions to speak with the librarian on his or her request for new books, you will be lucky to make it there. Someone will stop you in the hallway and want a few minutes of your time. You will finish the conversation, start toward the library again, and once again get interrupted. This will be a daily occurrence and something you might as well get used to. The important thing to remember is the original destination and the reason for it. Do not forget the librarian, and be sure you eventually make your way to his or her office.

It has been said that 30 to 40 percent of a principal's time is spent dealing with conflict. There are conflicts with principals and students, parents and teachers, teachers and principals, and community troubles that involve the schools. You must remember you are the leader, you make the decisions, and the end result of each conflict rests in your lap.

Unfortunately society these days can bring times of crisis and you may count yourself fortunate if you never experience such an incident. If you think dealing with bad media or an angry parent calls for communication skills, you have seen nothing compared to the skills that are needed to deal with a crisis.

On February 2, 1996, there was a school shooting in Moses Lake, Washington. March 13, 1996, brought a horrendous crime in Dublane, Scotland when 16 children and a teacher were killed. In Alaska on February 19, 1997, a principal and a student were killed by a 16-year-old. In March 1997 eight people in two schools were killed in Yemen. Between October 1997 and February 2008 there were at least 52 more crimes committed at schools across the world. These crimes do not include children who have been harmed or maimed by school bus accidents, injured in bus and car collisions, abused or seduced by sexual molesters, suffered from drug-related illnesses or death, as well as other horrible events that take place daily. Due to these inexhaustible incidents, you would be well advised to have a crisis management team. This team should have regular meetings and make decisions on how best to handle given situations. Establishing operational procedures and practicing crisis situations are only a few of the details this team should practice and plan for. It must be said that no matter how often the team meets or how many situations they try to prepare for, every imaginable crisis is different, and the factors that are involved in each situation will differ as well. Possibilities can be planned for; but every possible scenario cannot.

As a parent, I have witnessed how a community reacts to the death of student while in the school's charge. In our small town, such an incident happened during recess at a rural school in our district. The child chased a ball from the playground into a major highway, and was fatally hit by a semi-truck. I saw what a child's death can do, not only to the family and community but to the teacher in charge of the child at the time of the incident, and the principal in charge of the school. Believe me when I say, you most certainly want a team of people working to manage crisis situations.

Another problem in the schools is how everyone wants to put their new programs in the schools. "Everyone uses the schools as their own training area," said Barry Pichard. "Even the local politicians, police, fire, environmental groups, civic organizations, all have a school component of an essay, poetry, poster, banner, public speaking, etc., to get the schools involved in their effort or organization."

If we take the time to ponder Principal Pichard's words, we would realize this is a true statement. There are always "special programs" being brought to the schools by organizations, interrupting class and learning time. "Gun Control, bullying, sexual harassment, character education" are just a few of the special programs that Principal Pichard mentions. We have to wonder how this interruption might be more controlled. "Schools and the districts need to do a better job of screening all these requests so the teachers can do their job in teaching the students. Yes, many of these are important causes, but many of them are time consuming and are poorly organized, which is frustrating to the teaching staff, students and parents," said Principal Pichard.

In order to maintain good communication with the community, school districts welcome these special programs into the schools, never giving a moment's thought to the interruption and disruption of class time. When these programs are accepted into your school by the higher administration, you, as principal, are going to experience some frustration. As always it will be up to you to make the special visits work smoothly in order to maintain good communication with the community.

Dealing With Your Teachers

"Teachers make it happen or not happen," claims Principal Pichard. This is advice well regarded for first-year principals. Teachers are your go-between, and they make the learning part of education work. As a principal you are lost without them.

I asked John Fielding, principal of Idylwild Elementary School in Gainesville, Florida, "How important are your teachers?" His reply, "That's sort of like asking how important the sun, water, and food are to sustaining life." This was such a truthful statement that I knew it was well worth repeating.

Something you will want to remember — without your teachers there is no school.

The best way to deal with your teachers is to know each one individually. This is how you build relationships that will repay you in the long run. There are times when teachers are dealt with as a group, but to do so successfully you must know them personally. Talk to each one of them every day, even if it is only for a moment. By taking a minute each day to speak with each teacher you will learn their strengths and their weaknesses. You will get to know them a little more with each conversation, and you will get to know their talents, abilities, and needs. With the power of knowing each teacher individually you will have the power to know how to motivate them, and implement individual development.

Another way to gain successful communication with your staff is to share decision making. By involving your staff in decisions that involve them, they will be more inclined to do a better job; you are communicating to them that their opinions are important.

Always remember that people are creatures of habit and teachers are no different. Change is something people fear because it is unknown. If you make the change known before you implement it, most likely it will be accepted. Before marching into your new school and demanding your teachers implement a list of new changes, start small. If you work on one teacher at a time, and you do it right, change will become contagious and all your teachers will welcome the transition.

A place to consider suggesting new change is during your meetings after your observation of teachers. After you sit in a classroom and observe a teacher's method of teaching, you should schedule a follow-up meeting with him or her as soon as possible. This eliminates stress and worry the teacher may be experiencing due to having a new principal. Plus it is easier to remember everything that transpired during the observation; events will be fresh in your mind as well as the teacher's.

During the meeting it is crucial that the teacher feels as comfortable as possible, and the atmosphere is as informal as you can make it. There should be no interruptions unless it is an emergency. This assures the teacher that he or she has your complete attention; you are showing he or she is deserving of it.

Use an approach that is open and inviting by having the teacher convey how he or she feels the lesson plan went. Have the teacher express his or her view on how the lesson was accepted by the students. Self-reflection is good for personal growth, and oral self-assessment can cause one to realize important information that might otherwise be missed.

Once the teacher has finished his or her self-assessment, you may offer your own observations and candidly discuss the teacher's goals; whether he or she feels those goals are being met. Be sure to compliment the teacher and make recommendations if necessary. Ask the teacher what his or her feelings are on your recommendations and find a common ground.

Offering input, advice, and suggestions to someone for improving his or her work can create tension if done improperly. No one likes to be told how to do one's job. In fact many people will go out of their way to do the opposite if the assessment and suggestions are done in a less-than-diplomatic manner. By asking for a self-assessment, you give the teacher an opportunity to catch any possible mistakes or oversights. Discussing how the students absorbed the lesson gives the teacher a chance to recognize the possibility that the students are not responding, without your having to point it out.

You will want to keep in mind that not only is it important for new programs to be implemented, but that the programs be implemented for individuals as well as a wide range of educational needs.

In order to have your teachers be receptive to your suggestions for change, you must have good communication skills. You must always remember it is not so much what you say, but how you say it. Body language plays an important role when speaking to your teachers. If you are talking about improving lessons or improving teaching methods, body language is crucial to a successful meeting. If you ask the teacher to self-assess how the lesson plan was received by the students, and then gaze out the window while he or she speaks, the teacher will get the impression that you do not care. If the teacher has your complete attention, and you make eye contact, looking away only to jot notes on his or her opinions, he or she is going to believe you are truly interested, and you have a genuine desire to help.

Another way to implement a change that can grow into a huge transition is to focus on the teachers who develop projects and put them into action with their students. Some principals make the mistake of focusing on that one teacher who is revolted at the mere mention of something new. After thinking of that negative teacher, a principal may immediately give up on implementing changes. Instead of focusing on the negative teacher think of the teachers in your school who are upbeat and effective in student involvement. These are the teachers who can and will support your intuition and vision. Ask those teachers to come up with new ideas, implement them in their classroom, and then share the results with you. The results should, and will, become the talk of the day. The participating teachers will talk among themselves about the new changes, as well as to the other teachers about this new plan they are a part of. This is your opportunity to create a small buzz of talk in the teachers' lounge. Share the news about how these teachers did something wonderful in their class, and show enthusiasm over it. Once it becomes an accepted change by a few good teachers, ask them to take turns visiting one another's classrooms, sharing their ideas, projects, and results. When the mundane teachers see the buzz and excitement these new changes create, and they realize it is working to the advantage of the teachers involved, they will want to jump on board. Even the one teacher who is revolted by the mention of change will eventually come around to join in the celebration. No one likes to be left behind, not even an old, crotchety teacher who is too tired to welcome change.

One of the mistakes made by principals is not focusing on their best teachers. Some principals take the attitude that "they will be all right," and base their decisions on their mediocre teachers. This has the opposite affect of using the best tools available so your mediocre teachers will make improvements, and it does nothing for your best teachers. It is a no-win situation.

When implementing change, by focusing on your best teachers you will inadvertently press the average or mundane teachers to pick up their pace and do better. If resources are placed due to the best teachers' abilities, the other teachers will have to improve their skills to use the tools brought into the school. Why base new curriculums or new tools on average teachers when you can bring in curriculums and new tools that use the latest and best technology? The average teacher will have to bend in order to use the tools that will make his or her job easier in the long run.

By bouncing new curriculum ideas or other changes off your best teachers and getting their approval, you have a better chance that the rest of the staff will accept the change. These are the teachers who have the respect of the whole staff body, or at least the majority of them, and they are the key to acceptance from the mediocre teachers.

By making a new standard of sharing decisions on some issues with your staff, you may run into disputes. There are veteran teachers who are used to doing things the same way year-after-year, and have an aversion to trying anything different. They have taught the same curriculum, using the same methods, the same books, and the same droning voice for so long that they simply go through the motions. Many times they simply no longer have the energy or the enthusiasm to do things differently. Also you might run into barricades that are put in front of you by the school board or superintendent. Stand your ground and let it be known that this is your idea, your project, your goal, and your vision. The staff members who are enthusiastic will jump on board, and eventually, so will everyone else.

As a school leader you must balance guidelines and rules every day. There are times you will need to make exceptions, and situations will arise when you will be faced with a tough decision. Make your decisions based on your best teachers, and this will get you through the situations that need tough decisions. If you have someone in the school who is abusing a privilege, it would be a mistake to set a rule for everyone based on that one person. It is one person's lack of respect for school policy, not the whole teaching staff. Rather than set rules based on one or two people who ignore the rules, find out who those people are, and confront them on the issue. If you set a rule for all teachers based on one or two who are not following the guidelines, you are showing disrespect for those who do follow the guidelines. This is the same as teachers disciplining a whole classroom of students for the misbehavior of one pupil. It is not a fair practice, and you will lose the faith of your good teachers if you are not careful.

How you treat your favorite teacher or teachers also needs to be mentioned. In time you most likely will have at least one teacher who is fantastic at his or her job. This teacher might even be your advisor which is a wonderful asset. You must, however, be careful that you do not treat that teacher as special to the point of making him or her stand out. If you do some of the teachers may be envious, and possibly influence other teachers to distrust him or her. This could lead to the exceptional teacher being shunned by peers, and possibly cause your relationship with the teacher to be strained.

A common problem in some schools is placement of staff. You might find you have a teacher with exceptional skills and training in English, but is teaching history. This problem is out of control in some school districts. It is a waste of talent and skills. There are reasons, or excuses, why this situation has taken place.

In a school district I once worked for, I was told there were no job openings in the English position at the time of a teacher's applying for the job. Rather than lose a good teacher, she was placed as a history teacher until an opening in the English department was available. Ten years later the talented English teacher was still teaching history, and she was not a happy teacher.

Juggling the positions of teachers may or may not be feasible, but it is worth looking into. If a student attends college to become an English teacher, it is because that student has a passion for English. When the person finishes college and applies for a job, but is placed teaching a different subject, most likely he or she will not be happy and the students will not get the education they should be getting. By putting teachers where they shine, they will be happy and more productive. This is a sure bet on building a valuable team, and earning their respect.

The guideline of remembering to treat your teachers with respect seems to be the most common advice from the best principals. "I tell my teachers that a fair amount of my job is trying to keep the nonsense away from them. By nonsense I mean things like politics, silly rules handed down from on high, all the extraneous things that the outside folks think would be a wonderful idea for schools," said Principal Fielding.

If nothing else take from that quote just one part; the part about how he tries to keep the nonsense away from his teachers. In running interference Principal Fielding is protecting his teachers, and at the same time giving them the freedom to do their job: teach. While he deals with the "nonsense," the teachers can continue to do what is best for the students.

Teacher Conflict

The issue of firing teachers will be addressed more thoroughly in this section. It is a contradictory subject, and depending on whom you talk to, the conversation of firing teachers can be like throwing gasoline onto a fire.

If you take a moment to think of all the bad teachers you had throughout your school years, you might remember a few; possibly even three or four. Considering you had more than thirteen teachers, probably more than thirty, three or four is not too bad. The question, however, of why there were even three or four remains unanswered. Not only does the question remain, but it seems to be the focus of the media, parents, and nay-sayers all over the country.

According to John Stossel's report on *20/20, Stupid in America*, the teachers' union carries much of the responsibility for what is perceived as the problem of getting rid of bad teachers. In the same documentary, the teachers' union also is blamed for the failing of many schools. *Stupid in America* makes the claim that instead of protecting good teachers the teachers' union protects teachers who should be fired.

It is true that the firing of teachers can be difficult, and a long and costly process. There are times when the firing of a teacher can take several years. When a teacher is in limbo while waiting for a hearing on being dismissed, he or she still gets paid until there is a final determination. There are times a teacher does not "qualify" for being fired due to the contract he or she works under. When reading that a teacher may not qualify for firing under a contract, try to answer this question: Who agreed to this contract? Whose fault is it that this contract was signed? These are questions better left to communities and their school board. We are here to talk about how firing a teacher can be your problem, and how best to deal with it.

If you, as a principal, are in charge of a teacher who you feel is detrimental to the students' well-being, it is up to you to take charge of the situation.

As pointed out earlier it is easier and less costly to hire good teachers and build the foundation of your school from the beginning than it is to try to fire bad teachers. It is sometimes easier to attempt to help the bad teacher improve his or her skills than it is to fire the person. You can observe classroom activity, and conference with the teacher on the lack of his or her skills. You can coach, suggest, advise, and use instructional leadership until you are blue in the face. But there are going to be times when you may find a teacher who simply should not be in the profession of teaching. What then?

You are the only one who can determine whether or not a teacher is bad for your students. You are the one who must live with this knowledge, and face it daily. If you cannot find a way to improve the situation, you must be prepared for the possibility of being dragged across fire-hot coals. Ridding your school of a bad teacher is a long process that can lower school morale, make other teachers distrust you, pit your community against you, and have the media hounding your heels for anything that can be used as contradictory headlines.

When it comes to the possibility of firing a teacher, Principal Redd says, "Document, document, document. Meet, offer suggestions, and document some more." This is good advice when considering all the steps a principal and a district must go through to fire a teacher.

To cover yourself and to succeed in dismissing a bad teacher you must document all circumstances. Everything that has to do with your reason, or reasons, for trying to terminate a teacher must be documented, signed by the teacher, and placed in his or her file, and under the average contract you have 90 days in which to do it. More good advice on the possibility of having to fire a teacher comes from Principal Pichard. He says, "Never meet with a teacher by yourself... have another administrator in the meeting with you." If you have enough documentation accumulated in the teacher's file to justify an unsatisfactory evaluation, the matter then goes to a committee where a teacher can appeal. From that point on, the case is out of your hands and in the hands of the school's lawyers; unfortunately, the repercussions are not.

You can expect to have your motives questioned, your opinions battered, and your name smeared. Your school board and superintendent may be extremely upset with you, not because you are ridding the school of a bad teacher, but because of the bad exposure. The union newsletter will smear your name and the local paper may do the same. Every evaluation you do from that point on will be examined under a microscope, and you most likely will find that your colleagues will not wish to discuss the topic. In the end the cost of the hearing will be linked with your name, following you for months, and possibly even years.

On the opposite side of the spectrum, if the teacher is indeed a bad teacher who has had numerous complaints from parents, students have been yanked from his or her class and placed with a different teacher, and the teacher is dismissed due to your efforts, you may become the town hero. The sad truth of this scenario is that most likely you will not be hailed as the town hero until after the case is over; which could take up to a year or longer.

If you have a teacher who simply does not like young students and you realize the teacher chose the wrong profession, you may want to give the person support, some strategic training, and mentor him or her as you would your own child. To see this through you will need a truckload of determination and the strongest will you can possibly have, but sometimes it is possible to gently but firmly push someone to take a step in the right direction.

A teacher who is an under-performer may need nothing more than a little praise. Find something worthy to praise; it is in your best interest to do so. This may give the teacher the needed encouragement to strive for more praise which is exactly what you want to happen. Once this praise and the acceptance of it take place, the teacher most likely will have a small bit of trust in your opinion. This is the perfect opportunity to start an open dialog and receive feedback as well as give it. However a word of caution seems necessary here; tread lightly and do not move too quickly because that approach may make the teacher retreat and return to the normal distrust that is most likely his or her nature.

This is a good time to remind you of the communication skills we mentioned. This is where those skills come in handy, and make your job so much easier. Without good communication skills this strategy would feel like you are trying to muzzle a rabid dog. If you manage to get the teacher to participate in open dialog you have made an important first step. You now need to recall the practice of having your teacher self-assess. Ask him or her to tell you about an assignment, and what skills he or she is trying to emphasize. Ask how he or she learned this particular teaching method, and find a common ground on one or two goals he or she mentions while being careful how you say it. Deliver your message in a way that is clear and concise; remind the teacher that you expect some progress on these particular goals.

Another approach may be suggesting the teacher observe his or her peers. It is possible the teacher may discover a teaching method that is appealing. Chances are slim this will work, but it is worth a try. Then there is the "surround them with a strong team" approach. If you send a struggling teacher to a professional development program, you are setting the teacher up for several possibilities.

- Being surrounded by a quality team of teachers may instill a desire for the teacher to become part of this team.

- Taking part of the team's conversation after the program may implement the desire to improve his or her skills.

- Hearing the enthusiasm from the team of teachers may cause a seed of desire to sprout and grow enough to cause change for the better.

After the struggling teacher returns from the program, you may want to meet with him or her and discuss what was learned. I would suggest meeting with the entire team, and giving the enthusiasm from that team another chance to become contagious.

If after every effort the teacher does not show any attempt to improve, it is your moral and legal duty to inform the teacher of your decision, then document, get a signature, and file a report of inadequate performance. If you decide it is in the best interest of the students — and future students — to dismiss the teacher, then at the least be prepared. Keep in mind that even if the teacher has had a sexual affair with a student or has distributed drugs to students, there is no guarantee he or she will be terminated.

Please think about the last sentence you just read. A teacher who is guilty, or is allegedly guilty of having had a sexual affair with a student or having sold drugs to a student, may not lose his or her job. The teacher may simply have to move to a different town to teach. This fact is a thorn in the side of all good teachers. One bad person can cause many good people to be grouped and generalized. You would do well to remember this truth if you ever have an occurrence in your school where a corrupt teacher brings bad publicity to your doorstep. The morale of the staff and students will be low, and it will be up to you to motivate, encourage, and remind them of who they are.

When you become a principal you will either be a leader who has concern for yourself, or a leader who has concern for others. If you are concerned with only yourself, it will catch up with you, especially in the position of a school leader. The only way you can be sure your back is covered is if you run your school with the students as your top priority. If the students are not your number one concern, chances are you will have a failing school or there will be an incident that will take place and expose your failure as a leader.

When it comes to cleaning house and ridding your educational establishment of a teacher, or teachers, of bad repute, you are either up to the task or you are not. The dismissal of bad teachers is the ugliest part of a principal's job. Yet the hardest part of the job is living with the knowledge that you are allowing students to be subjected to someone who can cause a change in their future, a change for the worse. You need to ask yourself if you can you live with subjecting the students to someone they do not respect, and possibly receive ill treatment from. It is your decision, but first you should remember that you must live with yourself.

There are times when conflict within the schools comes from a distrust of the system, and there can be many reasons for this sentiment. If a new principal comes into a school, and runs the establishment like a dictator, there will be conflict. If a superintendent runs a district like a control freak who has spies placed in each system, there will be internal conflict. When a superintendent demands a principal tell him or her why a school is failing, there may be times the principal will point to the teachers and the teachers will point to the principal, causing more conflict.

There are many reasons for internal conflict, but even in the face of the school's personnel fighting internally, student education is still top priority. If you remain steadfast in this view you will find solutions to your problems inside the school. Treat your teachers as though they are important, which they are, and you will find ways to communicate, instill vision, develop trust, and build a team of exceptional educators.

It is imperative that you have your teachers make regular contact with parents. This builds trust between teachers and parents. It controls and addresses small problems that could otherwise become large problems. Some teachers may be reluctant to call parents for one reason or another, but getting them to do so is important, and is in the best interest of your school. If Johnny's grades are slipping or Sylvia suddenly becomes confrontational with her peers, a teacher will know there is something wrong. By calling the parent the teacher has brought the problem to the parent's attention, shown concern for the student, and given the parent a reason to trust him or her. The teacher most likely has taken action to address the problem helping Johnny or Sylvia show immediate improvement in behavior or effort.

The possibility of your teacher refusing to contact parents is indeed a problem. It most likely will begin as a small problem that becomes large and conflicting. Having an emotional parent burst into the office, demanding to see the principal, shouting obscenities, or making threats because he or she was not informed of his or her child's problem is going to be a day that you wish never happened; it is usually the end result of a teacher not contacting a parent. You need to find a way to make the most reluctant teachers believe that contacting the parents is beneficial to everyone in the school; then you need to find a way to have them act on that belief.

A training course on communication skills may be a small change you might want to consider. By teaching your teachers how to communicate, having them learn the proper words and the proper usage of those words, you are empowering them to communicate with parents, administration, their peers, and the community. Such training can only benefit your school.

You must have communication to find an instantaneous agreement in any situation of conflict. Communication facilitates a middle ground where both parties are willing to cool off and study the issue, or a long-term solution.

A scenario that came up during an interview with a school principal was consistent conflict between two staff members. This is a nightmare for principals who have had this experience. The following case study presents the veteran principal's experience and expert advice.

I called the two staff members into my office, and got them focused on what we were going to discuss. Then I said, "I am going to lunch duty now. When I come back to my office, I hope you two will have this worked out before I get back. The only way you can leave is if you settle this today. When I come back, if you are still here, we will continue to talk. If one of you is still here, then I guess we only have a one-sided issue that you can't get over. If both of you are gone, then this issue is settled and all of us can move on.'"

According to the principal, after lunch duty he returned to his office and found a note signed by both staff members. It stated, "All is well."

There will be times when you will be forced to play counselor for your staff, advising and guiding them in ways you never would have imagined. These are times that the schools cannot possibly prepare you for. The solution will be solved if you are a leader who knows his or her staff personally, a leader who has communication skills, and a leader who cares about his or her staff, school, and students.

Dealing with the Parents

According to Principal Barry Pichard, "Parents and the community expect schools to solve everything. Parents often expect the school to change their children because of their own bad parenting skills. Parents have changed dramatically in the last five years. Before, I would have some students who were rude and disrespectful to teachers and school staff, but now the students are taking their cue from their best teachers, their parents, because they see them being rude and disrespectful to school staff when they are at conferences and meetings." This statement is profound because it makes a statement not only about how a principal must deal with rude and disrespectful parents, but also how this change in society has had a trickle-down effect; it has altered the way each generation views authority figures and their peers, as well as how they treat authority figures and peers.

It seems the teachings from parents have fallen short and those inadequacies are now expected to be covered in the schools. This is more common in large cities, but the small towns and rural areas of the country are falling in close behind. What becomes a problem in some areas is when the rural areas or small towns and villages discover new curriculums that may be implemented, which does not set well in their local community. This situation has created problems for school districts and principals, opening doors to arenas that would have been better left closed. Now, however, the school principals in most locations are allowed to look at new curriculums, and decide what can and cannot be left out due to the community in which the students reside.

What are the teachers and principals expected to know, teach, and supply now that they were not before? Compared to as many as 20 years ago, there are many changes that have taken place in society, which means the schools have to change too. There are certain expectations of principals and school districts that were never a concern. In the past, a principal never had to worry about:

- Condoms

- Creationism

- Sex education

- Evolution

- Free breakfast

- Free lunches

- Inclusion

- Same-sex marriage

- The Pledge of Allegiance

- Death penalty

- No Child Left Behind Act

- Key kids

- School safety

- Standardized testing

- Accountability

- Funding

- Inequality

- Racism

- English

- Second languages

- Poverty

- School violence

- Student molestation

- Literacy

- Children raping children.

The list that principals must consistently consider could go on indefinitely. Fortunately for all of us our veteran principals have found a way to deal with this constant controversy and criticism.

Today's great principals view parents as partners, and most educational establishments benefit from this perspective when it is put into practice. Many times parent-teacher organizations and parent-teacher associations provide funding for school equipment, playground equipment, and various other necessities. Parents can be a tremendous asset or they can be a painful thorn in what might once have been a beautiful rose.

Parents rightfully deserve to know where their tax money is going, although some administrators are perturbed and perceive this as interference. Principals would be wise to treat all parents with respect, and there is good reason for this recommendation.

- The tax dollars of the parents' hard-earned money provides for much of your paycheck as well as the education of your students.

- Parents can and do volunteer for many events, relieving principals and teachers from long hours.

- Parent involvement can help boost morale.

- Parents can be your biggest fans and strongest allies.

- Word-of-mouth between parents travels faster than any other form of communication, and is good for public relations.

- Parents can save your job as well as make it easier.

- It is proven that involved parents produce excellent students.

- Involved parents support school programs.

- Positive relationships with parents influence relationships with students.

By showing an interest in the lives of students and their families you can make all the difference in how parents support the school district; and the parents are the ones who vote. On the other hand, principals must draw the line with family involvement the same as they must do with teachers and their personal problems. It is not wise to get involved in the personal problems of families any more than necessary. Where their problem, or problems, may interfere with the student's behavior, school work, or relationships with peers, is where the boundaries must be drawn. Beyond that it is wise to stay out of the mix. For instance it would not be sensible to play psychologist or lend a shoulder to a crying mother who is about to be divorced. But it is wise to keep an eye on that mother's child, and keep a list of neighborhood agencies on hand that can provide assistance.

A major consideration in dealing with parents is thinking in terms of handling a possible crisis. It would be so much better for parents to know that their children are in the hands of a principal they admire and respect when a calamity occurs. Another way to look at it is to think of your own children, or the children you plan to someday have, and think about how you want their principal to treat you as a parent.

Having good relationships with parents takes us back to communication. Parents or guardians usually get to know something about the principal through newsletters or other forms of communication from the school. If they come to an open house or parent-teacher conferences, they might meet you for a minute or two, but get nothing more than a first impression; although first impressions can leave lasting impressions. It is in your best interest to meet as many parents or guardians as possible at these events. Parents want the principal to be a part of the process. Most parents want the opportunity to communicate with the principal as well as the teachers. They need to hear about the achievements made by their children, not just the food fights during lunchtime.

When meeting with a parent over an incident involving their child, such as the aforementioned food fight, it would be wise to start the conversation by pointing out the good qualities of the student, and then dive into the bad news as gently as possible. After all you and the parents have the student's best interest at heart. If you treat everyone as though they are good people, they most likely will behave as such.

It is unfortunate that in the role of principal you could wake up any day to find your career in jeopardy due to one irate parent. This is something all leaders should keep in mind at all times. The threat of a parent raising a fuss about how their child was mistreated or wrongly suspended can hang like a dark cloud over your head if you let it. But, if you treat every individual as though they are good, chances are they will be, and you may never have to worry about such an experience.

There are parents who will have a distrustful or hostile attitude toward you before ever meeting you, and you most likely will detect this attitude on the initial meeting. It could be that the parent had problems when he or she was in school, or there was an issue with the previous principal. If by chance the parent comments on past problems, do not ignore his or her statements; instead acknowledge them and remember them. These are problems or issues that you have inherited, and only you can make it right. Let the parent know you were not aware of the problem; if you were aware of the problem discuss what you intend to do about it. It is possible these parents simply want to be involved but have been turned away. Attempt to involve them, and you may be surprised at how quickly their attitude will change.

There will be times when you see a parent come into school to pick up a student or drop off a lunch the student forgot. If you simply nod and keep moving they will be offended. Out of respect for the parents you should at least stop to briefly say "hello." If you do not know the parent you should introduce yourself, and be pleased you have established another contact who can possibly be an asset to your school. If nothing else you have made a good impression which is to your school's benefit.

If you treat everyone as though they are good, they most likely will be. This is true with all people you will have contact with as a principal. Teachers, students, and parents want to be treated well, and who can blame them? Let us say you have a student named Johnny. It is obvious Johnny is a rebel without a clue. You have learned through staff members and other students that Johnny's parents are divorced, his father is never around, and he lives in poverty; all too many reasons for his terrible attitude. If you treat Johnny's mom as though she is a worthless parent, she will have no reason to act differently. If you treat her with respect, and find good qualities in Johnny and mention those qualities, maybe she will strive to have better parenting skills; simply because she enjoyed being shown some respect. It is all in communication, respect, and attitude; the three fundamentals you will benefit from if you keep them on hand at all times.

Parents, teachers, and students are people, and all people like to be treated well. As we discussed previously, teachers who are treated with respect will strive to do better as teachers. The same holds true for parents. Make all communication as positive as possible, and focus on respect when communicating with parents. If you base decisions on good parents, you will gain many benefits, just as we suggested you focus your decisions on good teachers. In *What Great Principals Do Differently,* Todd Whitaker says that by focusing on bad teachers or bad parents when communicating with a group or an individual, you are making good people feel uncomfortable. If you are trying to make a point, wanting it to be known that you wish a belligerent parent would tone down his or her verbal abuse, you are going to fail. Instead of generalizing and including good parents in this announcement or speech, find a way to single out that belligerent parent, relieving the good parents from being added into a group in which they do not belong. Whitaker explained, "If applied consistently . . . who is most comfortable and who is least comfortable . . . it can bring simplicity to your decision on your approach. It is never the good parents or the good teachers that you want to make uncomfortable."

Let us look at the possible situation of a conflict that puts you in the middle of an angry parent and an accused teacher. We have stated that as a leader you should always stand behind your staff. This still holds true, but there is a right and wrong way to deal with the conflict of a parent versus a teacher. Even if you agree with the parent's complaint, it is in your best interest, as a principal, and the school as a whole, to back the teacher. However you need to assure the parent that you are sorry this misunderstanding has happened, and that the issue will be carefully considered and discussed with the teacher. With this approach you are not necessarily taking sides; you are assuring the parent, and at the same time backing your staff. If you do not back your teacher that teacher will lose trust in you and this could have a domino effect with your staff. If you have doubts about teacher's behavior or choice, it would be advisable to let the parent know that you will check into the situation thoroughly.

Please note that you should always follow up after stating you are going to check into an incident. Never forget to do this after you have verified the situation. This kind of dismissal will make you look as though you do not care. Such carelessness will be perceived as indifference by everyone, and rightfully so. If parents takes the time to contact you it is because they are concerned about their child. A parent's concern about a child's welfare should never be treated indifferently. After all that child is one of your students and the child's welfare is supposed to be your first priority.

Teachers are not always right, but they always need your support unless it is a situation or incident that is detrimental to the students. Such problems as parents versus teachers are usually limited if your teachers clearly know what you expect from them; another reason communication is so important.

Probably the saddest moment for a principal is when parent after parent come to his or her office, demanding to know why something is not being done about that horrible teacher who is dreadful with the students. How do you explain the truth? How do you try to make them understand that is it almost impossible to get rid of a bad teacher? How do you tell them that trying to dismiss a teacher is costly to the district? Can you say to a parent that the firing of a teacher will almost certainly cause low morale for the whole school and possibly taint your record as a leader?

You will never be able to just blurt out your feelings to a parent when facing this type of issue. The attempt to dismiss a teacher is complicated and the parents always want to know "why?" Many parents are under the impression that you do have control because you are the school leader, but it is a problem you have no control over. The truth is that your control is limited. If the teacher is bad for the students in such a way that it causes major problems in their education, it is up to you to decide what to do about it. There are still parents waiting for answers regardless of the problem.

We mentioned Mr. Waltin in Chapter Two, regarding his inability to deal with students, and also his anger management problem. The school principal had many parental complaints about Mr. Waltin, but a physical threat toward a student changed the issues and the principal was forced to make a hard decision. The principal took the issue to the superintendent. The teacher was removed from a teaching position, and put into a low administrative position. Was this the right thing to do? There are two ways to look at this issue.

First and most importantly the teacher was removed from having contact with students. Second, the teacher was not dismissed and the district saved a lot of money, as well as the other issues that arise with attempts to dismiss a bad teacher. It is important to say this again; the teacher was removed and put into a position where he would have no contact with students. As it should be, the first priority was the students. However this is only one side of the question on whether the final decision was the right one.

In this particular incident some parents would want to know why the problem was not resolved before physical contact with a student became an issue. Some parents would question if the leader should have done something earlier. There will even be parents who will state the principal is not a good leader because the problem existed for so long. Parents will wonder, and may even ask, how many students had their education corrupted, or interrupted at the least, due to this teacher not being dismissed earlier.

Another prime example of why parents sometimes have an attitude about school administration and their priorities was reported in *The Daily News*, on November 21, 2007. The news article related that a former principal had been removed from his post at Brushwick High School for failing to report a sexual assault to the police, and that he had been placed as assistant principal in Acorn High School in Brooklyn. This man, when principal, also had been disciplined for not immediately calling NYPD regarding a student who had a gun. One parent reported that she had been "put out of the school" because she did not have an appointment, and she was on the PTA.

Here we have parents with legitimate complaints plus schools that were issued the lowest possible marks by the Department of Education. Although these parents had good reason to be concerned about their children, it is unfortunate that they most likely will be distrustful of any principal or assistant principal who becomes the educational leader in the days ahead. Most likely, the parents will fall into the normal reaction of generalizing and distrusting any leader who follows the legacy left behind in these two schools.

There are always two sides to every story, and there will be conflicting opinions no matter the establishment, but in an establishment where there are numerous and varying factors, there will always be some conflict. It is important to realize that as principal you are the symbolic figurehead of the school. Your presence is expected at many events and you are the spokesperson for the staff, personnel, students, and sometimes the district. As principal you will interact with many people and how you treat them will be remembered, reported, discussed, and repeated.

We have already explained how important it is to meet the staff, personnel, students, and parents of your school. We think it is essential that you listen to all of these people and learn about their expectations. This will better enable you to deal with them as individuals which will be a tremendous asset on a daily basis as well as in times of conflict. If you are a principal in a diverse community, you are going to have more diverse opinions. If you are a principal in a rural area, chances are the parents will be more conservative, and less likely open to certain topics being brought into their school with new curriculums.

It has been noted that when teachers call parents out of concern for Johnny's slipping grades or Sylvia's sudden misbehavior, the rewards can be immediate and long lasting. By the teacher making the initial contact, there is not only a good result on behavior and effort on the student's part, but it shows the parent the teacher cares and has concern for the child's well-being. This concern builds trusting relationships. This kind of contact impedes a parent calling the school in an emotional outburst demanding to know why he or she was not contacted, and asking what is being done for his or her child. The same should be done by a principal. If you have discovered Johnny or Sylvia is having problems and the teacher has not contacted the parent, you should first invite the teacher to do so. Some teachers are reluctant to call parents, either due to a previously negative incident or simply because they are too stubborn. Regardless, it is then up to you to make sure the contact is made, eliminating what could be a negative conflict at a later date.

Like teachers, parents want to be informed. When they are not informed bad situations can arise, and incidents take place. These things make parents feel anxious, inadequate, and angry. Such emotions cause tension. When they are left out of the loop, and the loop is the circle that surrounds their child, they tend to become hostile. After all, it is their child who is the main focus here. Their child, along with the rest of the student body, is supposed to be the main focus of your job as well. There is more to being an excellent principal than simply putting the appropriate curriculums for the community into place. There is the well-being of millions of students at stake, and their future is not only in the hands of their parents, but also in the hands of our principals. It is up to you to make sure they are all right.

Some of the schools create a parent handbook as well as a handbook for the staff and the students. Handbooks can be beneficial to your job and help eliminate some problems before they have a chance to occur. Another way to cut the number of problems before they have a chance to arise is to inform the parents about their children's performance. Keep parents informed of:

- Student grades

- School policies

- Assemblies

- School calendar

- Special curriculums

- Standardized test scores

- Student behavior

- Change in curriculums

- Student progress or lack of

- Meetings

- Any changes in school policies and the reasons why

- Long-term substitute teachers

There are schools that run their establishment with the concept that parents are important partners. There are schools that have listed, in order, contacts parents should make with complaints or concerns. This list can be found easily on a school's Web site as well as in the newsletters that are sent home. Using a chain of command for concerns and complaints helps eliminate unnecessary objections or undue distress from entering the principal's office saving time for problems the teachers cannot solve on their own. If a parent has a conflict with the teacher, and he or she bypasses that teacher, it tends to make the situation worse. This action, when taken by a parent, can be construed as a lack of respect for the teacher. Setting the rule that parents with complaints or concerns should attempt to solve the problem by taking it to the teacher first, and then following up with the next level if necessary, you can stop problems from multiplying.

Parents are the same as teachers when it comes to following your expectations. They will abide by your rules if you make the rules clear and explain the reasons for your rules. By providing guidelines and defining your role as principal you are showing everyone respect, and asking for their respect in return. Remember — when you treat others as though they are good, they most likely will be. You will always have exceptions, but they will be few. Most parents have the same priority as you; their child's best interest.

Your Students

In 2000 the Department of Education stated that out of the 76.6 million students in the United States, 72 percent in the age range between 12 and 17 were academically on track, and over 85 percent of the adults in the United States had graduated from high school. The population over the age of 15 had a 98 percent literacy rate, but was below average in science and mathematics. The government stated that 85 percent of the students attended public schools, 1.7 percent was home-schooled, and one-tenth of the students attend private schools. That means there are numerous principals responsible for the education of over 76 million students. It means also that the majority of students are getting a fairly good education.

As a principal you realize that major educational issues center on curriculums, funding, and control. The No Child Left Behind Act is critically important because of its implications on funding and education. Funding for schools is complex, and the controversy over the No Child Left Behind Act is due to the act giving the Department of Education the right to withhold funding. If a school is failing, and the Department of Education determines your school, district, or even your state, is not making efforts to comply, they can withhold funding. Thankfully, most school funding comes from the state and local property taxes, but the bottom line is whether your students are receiving a good education.

Implementing good curriculums for students is probably the easiest part of your job once you get the teachers on board with the change. It is learning how to deal with many different people, on many different levels and with diverse views, and that can be challenging. Just like your teachers, your personnel, parents, and your administrative supervisors, students are people too. If you treat them with respect, you will get respect. If you treat them as though they are good people, they will be good people. If you let them know exactly what your expectations are, they will strive to meet those expectations. Young students as well as older students will follow the rules if they know what those rules are.

There are numerous ways to let students and their parents know what the rules are, and what is expected of them. You can use newsletters, student handbooks, post the rules on the school Web site, or hold a school assembly and invite the parents if you so choose. It is a good idea to let the students and their parents know what the consequences are for inappropriate student behavior or poor choices; however, the rules and consequences may be something you will want to word carefully. The reasons for this are quite simple; each student is a unique individual.

As a new principal it is high priority that you get into the hallways, the lunchroom, and the library to meet your students. Place names with faces and remember their names. It is all right to forget names for a while, but you must eventually know each one individually. Visit one classroom a day until you have been to all of them and have learned who your new students are. Greet them in the mornings, ask their names, and say good-bye to them when they are leaving in the afternoon. Make yourself visible and approachable to establish a relationship of trust and comfort.

I have personally known principals who invite students to the office just to visit. Your first reaction to this news may be, "Dear Lord, when would I have time to visit with students just to chat?" Yet a principal who makes time for visits, makes friends for life. These are the principals who are considered great leaders and leave lasting impressions. Moreover, by taking time to listen to what your students have to say, learning their views and opinions, and by responding to those views and opinions, you are building a trust that will not be broken easily.

Communicating with students is the best way to build trust. Whether you converse in the hallway or sit down and have lunch with them, you are building a lasting relationship and building trust. Students are invaluable in giving their opinions on school, and what is going on in the school. They are intelligent, and have information you cannot get elsewhere. It is important to remember that the students deserve the same respect you give to parents, the administration, and teachers.

As a principal you are going to hear many family secrets and information. You may learn a student's father is addicted to drugs, or the mother is an alcoholic. You may discover a child's custodian is in prison for molestation. There are things you will be told in the strictest confidence. While keeping the student's best interest at heart, you must never betray that confidence and trust. If you find it might be in the best interest to get help for a student, be sure to speak with the parent about this decision before you take action. There will be times when you are faced with turning a parent into the police or children's services. If this is the case be sure you are doing so out of concern for the child's safety, not for something you simply disagree with on a personal level. It is important to note also, that the privacy policy should always be maintained as well as the confidence.

If you take the time to wander the hallways and stop in a class here and there, you are going to learn more than if you visit only during scheduled classroom visits. You will learn more about the teachers and their methods of teaching and disciplining, in addition you will learn more about the students, their behavior, their attitudes, and their habits. While wandering around you may come to realize a certain student, named Charlotte, seems to be in the hallways more than in the classrooms. Why is Charlotte always in the hallways? You may discover that Charlotte is a top student in the school and the teachers send her to do their bidding because she is trustworthy and dependable. Now you have learned something about another student.

You will never completely rid your school of dilemmas. You will find solutions to some problems but problems will always exist. Sometimes the best we can hope for is being able to manage some problems and solve others. A principal must be cautious of certain dilemmas becoming common or regular practice making him or her calloused. When a student must be tested for learning disabilities, it might be routine for you, but the parent is anticipating a traumatic experience. When a student gets into trouble and a parent is called in for a meeting, it may be just another day for you as a principal, but it could be a first-time experience for the parent; it is extremely important to that parent but it may be emotionally disturbing as well. It would not be in your best interest, the best interest of the parent, or that of the student, to be monotone, cold, dispassionate, or indifferent. If you act in this way, you are being an uncaring, unprofessional principal who may never be a good leader.

As we have just shown you it is in your best interest to get to know your students as individuals. Another approach to having students behave appropriately, and strive to achieve good grades is using praise and rewards. If you give praise when it has been earned it will give the student good morale as well as the desire to continue striving for good grades. The reward approach, however, has been abused in some schools. The "praise and reward approach" is in somewhat of a debate as many schools have been using the approach in the hope that all students will try harder, even those who are doing just enough to get by. Unfortunately, this sometimes has an adverse affect. Will it have the effect to make students who do average or less want to do better or will they just continue with the status quo? If you reward students who only do average or less, will you belittle students who are hard workers and high achievers? If you are giving rewards to students who are high achievers, and students who are average or less, are you giving the less-achieving students a desire to achieve? If they are getting the same reward as the high achievers there is no motivation for them to do better.

Students who are praised in the classroom usually continue to show improvement and their morale also improves, as does the teacher's. However maybe the line needs to be drawn between teacher-to-student praise and rewards given at an assembly. To have a student bring his or her grade up from a D to a C is reason to give praise. The question still remains though whether the praise should be limited to teacher-to-student praise. At a school assembly, students are given certificates for being on the Honor or Merit Roll. Should students be given a certificate for having brought their grades up? Again, one must wonder if acknowledging students for valiant attempts to do better is in their best interest at all times, or just some of the time. Would it not be the same to reward a student for getting into trouble only five times on Tuesday instead of six times? According to Todd Whitaker's book, *What Great Principals Do Differently*, it is your job to understand what the deciding factors are and what is effective.

How you treat your students as a principal will determine whether they hold you in high regard, and whether they trust you. Picture a first-year principal standing erect in the hallway, arms crossed, staring at the students as though he or she expects one to pull a grenade from his or her pocket while they go to their lockers. The students are going to assume this new principal does not trust them, so they will not trust him or her either. On the other hand if the principal smiles and greets them, shakes hands with a few students every day, introduces himself or herself and asks their names, the principal is going to impress a hallway full of kids with his interest. One might hear a few snickers, but this will be because they are surprised by these unexpected actions. Some may even say the new principal is strange, and believe me, that principal will probably be acting strange in their eyes in comparison to their past experience, but they will soon come to realize that the principal loves the job.

By meeting and greeting the students, you are building relationships with your students, boosting morale, generating a positive atmosphere, creating trust, and showing the student body that you want to be a principal who is involved with his or her school. All of these things make a great principal in the eyes of students.

When you humiliate a student in front of his or her peers, you are causing psychological damage to that student, and to the rest of the students as well. When you intentionally cause someone discomfort, you are not only making enemies but you are making yourself look like a poor leader, and a poor example of an adult.

There is a lesson you can have your staff teach their students that will make life for the school so much better. The lesson is that it is important to make the best of any given situation. For example, you can dislike something but that does not mean you should show you dislike it or act disrespectful because of that dislike.

Just because a teacher is boring and loves to talk about the experiences he or she had rather than the lesson for the day, does not mean a student should go to sleep and show that they think the teacher is boring. The outstanding students may be bored to tears, but there still needs to be a respectful and interested looks on their faces. Some students will not learn this lesson at home. It is up to you to advise your teachers of this lesson, so they can teach it to their students. By teaching your students this valuable lesson, you are not only helping the environment of your school but you are teaching the students a lesson that will benefit them all their lives.

One point must be made here; there is absolutely no winning an argument with a student. Once an argument with a student has started the argument is lost. When you argue with a student you are no longer viewed as professional. In order to maintain the status of adult and professional you must never argue with a student. You may voice your opinion, but it should be done calmly and in a professional manner.

Student Discipline

When asked for suggestions in disciplining students, Principal Fielding said, "Consider how you would want it handled if your own child were in the situation." This is advice worth taking.

Let us consider two students: Johnny and Tom. Johnny has broken many rules over the past two years, since he entered high school, and seems to have an attitude that cannot be changed or improved. Johnny has been to the office numerous times, and has been suspended before. If Johnny threatens another student, he most likely will receive the harshest punishment noted in his handbook.

Tom has always followed the rules. He is a student who strives to stay on the Honor Roll, but happens to be experiencing a bad week. Tom has an altercation with Bobby, who is known to cause havoc every chance he gets. When Tom is called to the office, and you ask what happened, he explains that Bobby pushed him in the lunch line. Tom admits he pushed Bobby back after a personal insult was made about his sister, and then the fight started. You, as the principal, know your students, and you are surprised that Tom reacted to Bobby's taunting because Tom normally would laugh it off and ignore it. You ask Tom if everything is all right or if there is something bothering him because you know this is not like him. This is when Tom breaks down and tells you that his parents are getting a divorce. What you do at this point that can make a difference in Tom's life, not just as a student, but as an adult also. Remember the adults who have an attitude toward you before they even meet you due to a bad principal when they were in school? We do not want Tom to become that kind of adult. Therefore, the question is whether you give Tom the harshest punishment or go easy on him due to the stress he is under.

Leaders that know each student individually, know when to make exceptions. If Tom would normally handle a situation like this with ease, but is having a hard time at home what are you to do? You also realize that when there are family problems even the most irascible siblings immediately feel protective toward one another. This would explain the reaction to Bobby's insult toward Tom's sister. However, the problem remains that there were at least 100 students who saw Tom's reaction to Bobby's insult. Those 100 students know the rules and expect there to be some kind of consequence. If you do not give a punishment chances are it will come back to haunt you in due time. You can go easy on Tom and tell him, "Because you are normally a good student and you are having some difficulties, I want you to make a visit to the counselor to talk to him."

By making an exception you have left Tom's respect for his school and his teachers intact. You have let him know that you feel he is a good person and a good student. You have given him a consequence that is not the harshest punishment because of these reasons. At the same time you have given him an opportunity to speak with the counselor, which may help him through this trying time. You have also thwarted any argument that Tom did not get punished for his actions, possibly saving yourself some future problems. This is why your wording in setting down rules and consequences must be carefully introduced. Every situation is different just as every student is different.

Students may not have the ability to decipher and deal with all situations, but they know right from wrong. It would be foolish to give them any less credit. By being a good principal and handling Tom's actions, giving a lesser punishment, your student body will be relieved. They are smart enough to realize Tom broke the rules, but they are also smart enough to know that Tom is normally a good student, and should not be punished as harshly as others might have been. This is good judgment on your behalf, as well as a surefire way to keep the student body on your side. If you had suspended Tom a large portion of the student body would have immediately formed a bad opinion of you; an opinion that would include mistrust.

There will be times when you will be able to bend the rules for the best of the student, and it is done in a way that does not harm the school's best interest. This is the case with our previous example of Tom. There will be times, unfortunately, when you will not have such an easy decision. If you ask yourself what is best for all the students, it may sometimes require consequences you dislike having to implement for one or two students. What if Tom and Bobby were good students who never caused any problems unless they were in the same room? For some unknown reason, their personalities clashed, and they rubbed one another the wrong way. Every time they saw one another in the hallway or at a football game, they ended up in a fight. What would you do as a principal? As an effective principal you would most likely have to send Tom and Bobby to different schools. You wouldn't be able to keep one at your school and send the other away, because that would not be a fair decision. On the other hand if you sent Tom away and not Bobby, then Tom's friends would lose trust in you as a leader, which means it would not be fair decision to the student body as a whole.

If you think back, can you remember a time when you were treated inappropriately? If you have ever experienced it, you will remember. The same holds true for mistreating students. You are an adult and you chose your career. While we might excuse Tom for his inappropriate behavior due to his parent's divorce, no one will excuse you for screaming at a student who is running in the hallway. You must maintain a calm demeanor , at all times, and an optimistic attitude. If students witness their principal screaming at one of their peers, or at one of their teachers, it will cause conflict, humiliation, embarrassment, a bad atmosphere, distrust, and dislike. Your job will become hell as well it should. Always treat your staff and students with respect, and you will be rewarded tenfold. To be a great leader you must lead by example.

There will be times, more often than not, that you will think you can finally grab a minute of peace and quiet. You make your way to the office only to find a group of students waiting for you. You discover they had a spitball fight during class, and the problem, as well as the outcome, has been put in your lap.

Many questions will come to your mind before you even begin to get inside the door: Are these kids usually troublemakers? Is the teacher who sent them here one of those who is intolerable of problem students or a teacher who does not deal with dilemmas, choosing to hand it over to the principal in every instance? Are any of the students known bullies? Will there be meeting with a belligerent parent no matter the outcome?

All of these questions and more will help in determining the outcome of this conflict. There are no problems that are exactly the same, just different students. You have a school full of individuals, all having special personalities who are worlds apart in their tolerance level. With so many students in one building there are bound to be conflicts, but being able to manage them is the idea — not necessarily solving them. If you can manage conflict, you need not worry so much about the solutions.

According to Principal Fielding, "Conflict, unfortunately, seems to be inevitable in this job. If it is with the kids, the rule is: 'You tell me your side, and the other does not interrupt. Then we switch, and if the stories match, we figure out what to do to fix it and go back to work. If the stories do not match, we start over until they do.' "

By putting the rules on the table at the beginning of the meeting, Fielding let the students know there will be no tolerance for lies. The consequence will be sitting in the office until the truth, and only the truth, is told. There are many good reasons for this rule. It gives the students reason to pause in their thinking. It gives them notice that the situation can be easily resolved if they are honest. It gives them assurance that their principal is willing to listen to both sides.

One must remember Principal Fielding has already built the relationship he needs with his students for a foundation of trust to be prevalent. Trust will open doors and bring forth honesty faster than threats or yelling. Trust is the key ingredient in dealing with student conflict. As Principal Fielding likes to say, "Of course, the best advice (in dealing with conflict) is to try to find ways to avoid conflict."

Some students are immature and this can cause behavioral problems. Also inclusion, mainstreaming special education students with regular students, can cause conflict. There are racial issues, and dilemmas in the homes of the students. Low self-esteem is regularly a reason for bad behavior. Some students have anger management problems. A student may cause mayhem because of boredom. There are times students will cause problems because the teacher has no management skills in her classroom. All of these possibilities are factors that cause problems. If you know your students you will have the insight to manage the conflict, and know whether or not the problem can be solved.

When dealing with young students you should bear in mind they need structure and routine. If they do not have these disciplines in their homes, they may not go along with them too well at school in the beginning, but in time they come to realize that structure and routine mean security and dependability. By having structure and routine some behavioral problems may be eliminated. When you deal with young children because of misbehavior, make it clear that it is the inappropriate behavior you are disappointed in or objecting to, not the child.

If you have a staff that shows mutual respect for one another as well as to the rest of the personnel and the students you will have reduced the discipline problems. This will hold true for schools that house all ages. Setting rules and explaining them will also help eliminate discipline problems.

If every person in your building feels valued as an individual, you have paved the way for an atmosphere that will be inviting, cheerful, successful, and orderly. This atmosphere will give students a sense of pride in their school and in themselves, and it will reinforce acceptance of rules and expectations. Students will respect the leadership of a positive principal who is highly visible, greets the students each morning, and bids them farewell each night. If you must attend a meeting and cannot be there to greet them in the morning, you will be missed, and that is a positive reaction to your absence. You must have a clear and precise policy of discipline, while remembering and reminding the teachers that each student and each incident is unique. Each problem will need to be dealt with differently while maintaining respect and expectations for and of the students. In doing this you will stop potential problems before they occur.

If you have a policy in place defining how problems are to be dealt with fewer problems will end up at your door. Post your policy in the student handbook and in newsletters and announcements that are sent to the parents. Finding solutions to conflict and concerns should start on the level where the problem exists. If there is no solution agreed on, it should then be taken to the next level. Procedures for parents dealing with complaints and concerns should be in this order:

- With the teacher or subject manager

- The principal

- The superintendent

- The school board.

The procedure for student conflict should be handled a little differently, and also noted in the student handbook, parent handbook, newsletters and announcements. The procedure for student conflict should be as follows:

- Schedule a face-to-face meeting with the teacher and student

- All students involved in the conflict will meet with the teacher

- Students will follow advice of the teacher through a process to resolve the conflict

- Students will make an agreement with the teacher on behavior

- The teacher will contact parents

- As a last resort, the students will be sent to the principal's office.

Placing this procedure in the handbook as well as in newsletters, announcements, and on the school Web site will eliminate the amount of complaints you, as a principal, will have to deal with. It will show that you trust your teachers to handle the problems with their students and parents as they arise. You should never take it for granted that your policies are being followed. Always check with your teachers to be sure parents are being informed, students are being taken care of correctly, and conflicts are being managed.

Many principals advise a "cooling down" period for students before you try to talk to them about the problem especially in the matter of a fight or an argument. Giving a student time to calm down is extremely important.

Trying to speak with an angry or emotionally upset student is like asking a poisonous snake if he wants a hug then quickly moving in to wrap your arms around his neck. One principal states it is wise to "make sure you have the entire story before proceeding with any discipline."

According to Principal Pichard, "Discipline is probably one of the hardest things to do because you have the final word on whether a student stays in school, is suspended, or expelled. Discipline, or should I say good discipline, involves counseling and time. The time spent with a student or group of students may limit the time you have to spend with them in the future about the same issue or situation."

Taking the time to know your students as individuals, knowing their circumstances, what kind of students they are, and where they come from all plays a part in how discipline is shelled out and how harsh it will be. "When you think you have the entire story you look at the puzzle and see what the picture really looks like. Sometimes it comes together . . . and is clear and concise. Other times it looks like some old puzzle that has a few pieces missing and you will never find them," says Principal Pichard. "Discipline [is] probably the most time consuming and worst aspect of the job."

The principal managed to get a clear and concise picture from Tom by talking with him and finding out his parents were getting a divorce; the principal found the missing puzzle pieces. When it comes to the old puzzles with missing pieces that are never found, you will find there are times when you must go with your gut instinct. Just remember Principal Pichard's words of wisdom when he says, "Every disciplinary action does not need a consequence after you have investigated thoroughly." Again with our student, Tom, there may be times when you will decide to bend the rules because you know it is in the best interest of the student and the student body as a whole.

Your Community and Public Relations

In order to be a good principal, or at least an accepted one, you must be a people person. The majority of your time will be spent interacting with people from all stations in life: parents, students, administrative supervisors, business people, staff members, vendors, and community members. You will be asked to speak at special functions and events as a representative of your school. These occasions are important and to do this successfully you will need to know your community, how to communicate with the public, and how to interface with groups and individuals.

Your community is made up of the parents, the administrative supervisors, and other members of the neighborhood. In order to better understand your school, you need to understand the community, know what their expectations are, and learn how they view their school. You will find that certain groups have specific expectations. Parents expect their children to be safe and well educated. Community members expect the school board to work with them on procedures and disbursements. Your supervisors gave you a list of responsibilities when they hired you, and they expect you to carry out those responsibilities thoroughly and appropriately.

In looking at these expectations you will need to determine if they are feasible, especially as you look at each group's expectations individually and then as a whole. If they are not possible, it is up to you to find a way to convince one or more of the groups to change or alter their expectations; otherwise, you will lose their support and can expect conflict on the horizon.

In mingling with the people of your new community, you need to maintain a positive attitude. Smile and greet them, introduce yourself and ask questions about the community. Get to know them personally. Observe how they react to you as principal and listen to what they have to say. Invite them to school functions. Assure them that they are welcome to visit the school at any time to see the school community in action.

You will want to know the history of the school, and how that history affected the community. There are many facts about the school and its relationship with the community that you will want to discover. Due to financial hardships some schools have been forced to merge which often creates dissimilar groups inside the school and throughout the community. You will want to ascertain whether there have been resolved or unresolved school-community issues. If the school has a bad reputation within the community, what is the reputation built on — fact, bad public relations, gossip? You will find this information in your own backyard at neighborhood churches, hair salons and barber shops, grocery stores, hardware stores, gas stations, restaurants, and even flower shops. People love to talk, and once you get them to open up you will gather more information than you ever dreamed possible. Go to the markets, the malls, local eateries, and ball games and mingle with your neighbors. Visit all these places, listen to their concerns, and learn about their customs and beliefs. The best way to get along with people, and win their support is to get to know them.

You will need to look at the school district and understand where the money comes from. Are there more parents in the community than there are senior citizens? Even if the majority of people are parents, is there a large percentage of senior citizens? If so how could you get them involved with your school? If the parents have been shut out and turned away over the years how can you win their trust and get them involved with their children's education? Are there ethnic groups in your community, and are the students from those groups being educated accordingly? Are you now residing in a blue-collar town or a white-collar city?

These are questions you will want answers to in order to do your job appropriately. Community plays a big part in how the schools fare, so it is up to you to get to know your community's needs and expectations.

Where do you come from? What is your background? Do you "look" like you will fit in with your new community? The answers to these question will determine how some people in the community receive you. If you are now in a rural setting after having lived and worked in a big city, chances are there will be several residents who will not trust you or your judgment. The same is true if you hail from a rural area and take on a job in a big city; many groups in the community will expect you to fail.

You will want to get to know your community leaders. Find out if the town or city is run by a mayor, city council, a charter, or some other type of city government. Visit the chamber of commerce and introduce yourself. Tell them about your vision for the school. Let the people of your community know you want only what is best for your students and their future.

Excellent communication skills and good public relations tactics are needed to address the cost of education so frequently seen in news headlines. It is important that you are a person with a good attitude and a positive approach. When parents feel they are not wanted in the schools, or they are too time consuming or a nuisance, you are going to create a community of distrust. A suspicious community will pounce on any little error and make it seem as though you are not doing your job; that you are not fit to be the principal.

In a nearby community where I worked the schools used to send a letter home before the teacher-parent conferences. The letter suggested that parents who had good students should not make an appointment with the teachers, leaving time for parents and teachers who were having difficulties with their students. How do you think this made the parents of good students feel? Although it is understandable that problem students require more time for teachers and parents to confer, it is not a good idea to turn away the parents of students who excel. Even if the parents just want to schedule an appointment to tell the teachers thank you for doing a good job, you are taking away time those parents want and deserve, and you are taking away from the gratitude your teachers may seldom hear from parents. If you as a principal feel there is a need for more time for teacher-parent conferences to develop a plan to help the students who are misbehaving or pulling bad grades, then maybe you could consider scheduling a night for parents of excellent students to come in and meet with the teachers. By pushing away parents from either kind of student, you are creating bad community relations.

A good practice for developing good community relations is having days when parents and the community are invited as visitors to sit in during class and observe. You could do this on special occasions: a day when shop class is building something special for the school, or when the oceanography class is setting up a new aquarium.

You will find a multitude of ideas for parent and community involvement at the PTA or PTO meetings. Plan to speak at one of the meetings and ask for ideas that would involve the community with the school. Let the members know you want to involve the community, and you will have begun laying the foundation for a great, future relationship with them.

There are many things you can do as a principal to get your community involved with the schools. The days of picnics and school fairs have mostly vanished, but there are many communities that would love to see those times of school-community return. If you decide to do something of this nature, you should invite all of the community, not just the parents. Inviting the community to help is the best way to get them involved. You could distribute flyers, have the local newspaper write an article about the events and explain where the money will go, and place invitations in the newspaper and at the local library. There are many ways to improve school-community relations, and what you get back could be well worth the effort and the time you put into it.

In working with the community and involving them in the school, you are using wise public relation tactics. There are many clubs and organizations that are more than happy to work with the schools and help students who need it; but do not use them merely to help needy students. It is best to involve them in good times and happy events also. Kiwanis, Rotary, Lions Club, and First Book are all organizations that can and will get involved if you simply invite them. Local businesses also like to be involved with the schools; it is good public relations for them as well. There was a program in our district where local business became partners with a school. They helped with volunteers, resources and even monetary needs. Many businesses and organizations feel a sense of pride when they become involved with the school. Sometimes the student's parents are employees making it even more important to them and their employers.

Letter writing is another form of good public relations. This is almost a lost art, and few administrators take the time to do it. Communication has become cold and impersonal with e-mail and fax machines. By writing letters you are making a statement of how important the recipient is to you. You are taking the time to write the letter, address the envelope, and put it with the mail to be delivered. This is a bold statement that says you feel they are worth the time and effort. It is in your best interest to communicate through a letter whenever possible. Even form letters are more personal than e-mail or faxes. Newsletters are a type of form letter, but the communities love to receive them because it keeps them informed and involved in their children's education.

You may want to consider having your staff learn good public relations and communication skills as well. There will be times they will need good skills in these areas, and teacher-parent conferences are a good example. Regardless of how many ways you find to communicate with the community, informal communication generally is the most effective. Instruct your teachers and staff in good communication techniques, involve them in school and keep them informed. Surveys indicate that school employees are the most reliable sources of information. Without effective public relations, you are not going to have good school-community relations and community support; it is always in your best interest to use good public relations techniques.

If you are not already, you will want to make sure you keep the school and the community informed of programs, special events, activities, and other school functions. This is good public relations, and if you do not do this, you will forever be marred in the community in which you work, and so will your school. Make the school calendar public by placing it on the school Web site and in newsletters. There are other pieces of information that should be community knowledge as well: staff information, emergency closing information, parent associations and contacts, homework policies, the school's schedule, procedures for registration, testing dates and programs available to students, and discipline policies. Many schools have found it is advantageous to make a parent handbook like the student handbook. This will help eliminate phone calls for information, and at the same time give the parents quick answers to questions. Some information should be shared with the whole community, and there are other ways to do this.

Once you know your staff and your community, you will discover there are valuable resources for public relations in your building, and outside your building. There may be a well known teacher or parent who is popular and visible in the community, and he or she would be an asset at public functions and presentations. These are the people you need to have on your side; they are your contact people. Once you know who they are communicate with them. Build a relationship of trust with them and keep their contact information close at hand. These are the members of the community and the school that can keep you informed of whether a rumor is true; if there is something going on with your students that you should know about; whether there are issues being discussed in the community that you should know about; or many other simple issues that you may have overlooked or not been aware of. These are important people to know, and you would bode well to figure out who they are as soon as possible.

There is one piece of advice we must pass along to you at this point: in order to maintain a good relationship with your community and have good public relations with your neighborhood, you must first begin to establish one inside your school. The best place to start would probably be with your parent-teacher organizations or associations. Letting these parents know you want to work with them, that you are opening the doors to good relationships, and the word will spread. If you can, it would be advisable to meet with the president of the committee before each monthly meeting or at least quarterly. Even if you have a teacher represent the school and attend meetings, it is prudent for you to meet with them personally once in a while.

Getting the parents involved in school calendars, school events, newsletters, and other programs is good public relations, but many principals are hesitant to do this. The more input you have on how to do something, the more chance there is for conflict. Some principals shy away from getting parents too involved because of conflict and do not consider the benefits. However, it bears to mention that for some principals it simply is not worth taking the risk. It is up to you to make the distinction: conflicts or benefit.

Being visible in your community is the first step in becoming accepted as part of the community inside the school and out. If you are visible, it is a way of saying you are also available. It is obvious that you cannot always be available at the drop of a hat, but when parents or community members come calling unexpectedly, it is advisable for you to make yourself available if you possibly can. If you cannot it is important that your office staff know to relay this message and explain that you will be more than happy to meet with them if they will schedule an appointment. Again, having your staff learn good communications skills is worth considering.

Another approach to good communications and public relations is the idea of taking the time to call parents to share good news about their child or children. If a child is chosen to receive a presidential award, what better way to find out than to have the principal call to deliver the good news? It will take all of three minutes to make the call, and that is three minutes well spent. Imagine, if you will, how many phone calls that parent will make after you hang up. Then imagine how many people that parent will relay this story to at the grocery store, the hair salon, and at his or her job.

As stated before always meet with parents when they request it and be sure to listen to their concerns and complaints. If you are viewed as a good listener and a principal who makes suggestions as a way of solution, then you are going to receive high marks in the course of "Acceptance in the Community."

How you are perceived by the community will determine the image of your school in the eyes of the community unless your school's image has already been tarnished or is unblemished. You may walk around your school and attempt to look at everyone and everything you see objectively, but this is not always easy. If you listen, however, to what people are saying to one another and to you, and imagine what someone else would think if they heard the same things you are hearing, you may get an objective point of view about how your school would be viewed by an outsider.

Stay on your staff and have them help you to keep a positive attitude and upbeat morale inside your school as well as outside the building. This is imperative in good community relations and good public relations. The more positive you and the staff are the more positive the students will be. It will have a domino effect becoming contagious to the students, to the parents, and then the rest of the community.

When I worked with the parent-teacher organization, we were allowed to use the bulletin board in the main hallway by the school entrance. We worked out a plan with the teachers and would visit a few classrooms taking candid photos of the kids with their teacher. These photographs were developed and put on the bulletin board every two weeks and the idea was a smashing success. The students loved seeing their picture and pictures of their friends, and the teachers, the principal, the parents, and even the superintendent thoroughly enjoyed seeing the smiling faces of the students in their school environment. Something as simple as using the bulletin board for student photographs can boost morale 110 percent and it makes for good community and public relations.

I am ending this chapter with a quote from an exceptional principal, John Fielding. It is food for thought and advice well worth taking. "These days, public schools are under attack from all sorts of places and that requires us to be a bit proactive in getting out the good news. If your school has special programs or exciting things that may be out of the norm, or staff that do something outstanding, these are the things you want to share with the media."

6
CLOSING THE GAP

———

While doing research and interviewing principals I realized the advice, stories, questions, answers, and suggestions for your job could be endless. Due to the overwhelming responsibilities, and the various veins of tasks that stem from those responsibilities — which are too numerous to even list — I had to remind myself to stay on topic. A stopping point had to be made, a line drawn in the sand, and staying on the topics of necessity had to be enough. If I tried to follow all those veins, those endless tasks and duties, there would be no end to this book, and the soon-to-be principals who read it might run fleeing from the campus grounds, screaming at the top of their lungs. We need great principals; therefore, I must try not to scare you too needlessly.

We have seen the hiring and firing of teachers, the implementation of new curriculums, the need for slow change, and the best way to make those changes. We have observed the need for discipline and the way exceptional principals have dealt with it. The eyes that are always watching you have been discussed, and the parents who want excellence from you have been placed where they fit best for your school. Throughout all this discussion, however, we have not yet talked about you personally.

You are going to experience many changes in your life once you become a principal. You may have experienced some of these already, but there are more to come. The need to do your job, and to do it well may make you become fixated. You may lose sight of your personal life, as well as what it was like before you became a principal. It will take work, patience, management, and a lot of courage to meld your previous life with your current life. We are going to help you do this.

First, before we delve into what is happening in your life, we are going to discuss a subject that deems important enough to re-examine: The Media.

> *"Be open and honest. Be careful! Some reporters are just looking for a negative story. If you find someone like this then avoid them."*
>
> **Principal Robert Spano,**
> Naples, Florida

The Media

We have discussed how the media can seem like the hounds of hell on your heels if you are not careful. So, this is one area we need to scrutinize closer. A crisis management team seems to be the normal thought pattern for most schools since the mass killings at Columbine High School in 1999, but no matter how carefully you plan, you can never prevent every possible threat. When horrible and senseless incidents take place, the media will be all over you, your school, your students, your staff, and the parents. They are looking for that one word or sentence that will be featured in the headlines for days, weeks, or perhaps even months. Most reporters still have integrity and want to do a good job of reporting the news. But I can tell you from experience that it is not the reporter who has the last say on how his or her article will be printed. Nor does he or she have the last say in whether the story is told and then put to rest. It is not the reporter's choice to decide if a story is to be revisited like the grave of a decaying corpse.

Due to the fierce drive for shocking news, when a crisis does erupt, it would be in your school's best interest to have an idea of how you and your staff will handle the situation.

In Chapters One and Two, we briefly touched on the importance of your getting to know your building. It is advisable that you know the layout of your building before school starts. If, by chance, you start the job in the middle of the year, get to know the building as soon as possible. In addition to knowing every inch of the building, you want to know the grounds and all surrounding buildings also.

If your school already has a crisis plan in place — learn it — all of it. Know it inside and out, backward and forward, and walk the buildings and the grounds with the crisis plan in hand. It also is a good idea to walk the buildings and grounds with a blueprint in hand. Learn every light and light switch. Know which alarms exist, and where every one of them are located. You also must know the location of your fire extinguishers, evacuation routes, and the location of all building shelters.

Obviously, you want to know all of these things for the safety and security of your students and staff, but there is another reason to have this knowledge. You will want to know all of these measures of security by heart because of the media as well.

Imagine this scenario if you will. You are at a state-mandated meeting and, as usual, the most boring speaker was saved for last. You have been sitting in silent misery for five hours, and all of you, teachers and principals alike, has finally been released. You are mingling, allowing the blood to once again circulate in your legs, sharing jokes and laughing gaily with a few members of your staff. A young, self-assured gentleman approaches confidently, and joins in the discussion. You notice he is wearing one of the familiar name tags just like the one that has irritated you all day, but you cannot make out his name or district due to the tag having flipped over. The discussion turns to a recent school shooting in another state. The crisis ended badly due to human error. In the middle of the conversation, this young man leans over and asks, "You are a principal aren't you? How would you have handled the situation? How would you have evacuated your students?"

If you do not do your homework, you will end up looking like a fish out of water, flopping on the shore in total confusion. However, this is our scenario, so we are going to say you did your homework, and you do know your stuff. You take a deep breath and confidently spout off the most effective crisis plan for this type of incident, explaining how you would effectively handle such an emergency, and how your students and staff would evacuate the building, or lock down and stay put. Later as the young gentleman prepares to leave, he reaches out to shake your hand and his name tag flips over to reveal that he is a reporter for a local newspaper. Although you know you expelled the appropriate response for the crisis, you begin to sweat, your heart pounds with worry of whether you said anything that could be taken out of context to become the next headline.

This is a small, but possible, example of how fast a story can turn into a disaster for any school, and school leader. This is why it is imperative you know your school inside and out.

Another suggestion is that you take the time to meet the police captain and the fire chief. They are remarkable assets to your community and your partners in the safety of your school. A good way to establish a relationship is to pay them a scheduled visit, and ask if they would personally take the time to go over the crisis plans and evacuation routes with you. This not only begins a new and important relationship in your community, but it helps you gain needed assurance of ascertaining the safety of your students and staff. The input and knowledge from fire and police leaders is invaluable. If you can get them to attend a crisis management meeting you have gained priceless information and advice.

As a first year principal be forewarned; an occurrence at another school, be it a school shooting, the molestation of a student, or a misunderstanding that causes a student to be expelled erroneously, could swamp you with calls or e-mail from parents and local newspapers. I would like to share a story with you that will exemplify this statement.

Principal Barry Pichard brought it to my attention that an incident which happens elsewhere can cause a swarm of phone calls, e-mail, or visits from parents. He explained how such an incident happened to him: "Another Sunrise Elementary school in Florida had a student who brought a knife to eat her lunch. At that school they suspended the student and it went on TV with the news report. A few days later I get these interesting e-mails from concerned citizens condemning my school for disciplining this student."

Being a veteran principal who is aware of the importance of public relations, and the backlash that could take place if the e-mail went unanswered, Pichard went on to say, "I did respond to all the concerned citizens, letting them know that they had selected the wrong Sunrise ES. I told them the positive things about our school and also cc'd my Superintendent, Area Superintendent and the Public Relations Director."

Not only did Principal Pichard take the time to respond to the citizens, he kept the administration informed of what had happened and how he had handled the situation. This is a perfect example of, not only a veteran principal, but a worthy leader.

It seems much of our media reports only the negative aspects of a school, creating a fear that is internalized by millions of parents. Many times these reports will destroy a school's reputation. It is seldom that you find positive reports of a school in a newspaper or on television. Drugs, rape, violence, and sexual molestations are the headlines we see and hear in the media when schools are mentioned. There have been so many hyped reports of drugs and violence that some students say they are afraid to go to school.

In Stossel's *20/20* report on the failure of public education, he criticized public schools and created a segment which leaned heavily in favor of vouchers and charter schools. The argument was for vouchers intended to force public school improvement. But one has to wonder — if funding is already too miniscule for public schools, how is taking money from public schools to help students attend private schools going to improve education? Once again public schools were made to look alike failures by Stossel's report. As a reporter, Stossel failed miserably, but most reporters do today, simply due to the fact that both sides of the story are no longer represented equally. I feel it is my duty to point out that most reporters do not have the last say in how their articles will read or what portions of a televised taping will be cut.

In June 2007 **WashingtonPost.com** printed an article which dragged Washington DC public schools through the mud. It was reported that more money was spent to run the schools, going to administration, than money spent on teaching. While it may be true there are schools in Washington DC that are doing poorly by the students, the question remains, "Are all the public schools in Washington DC failing the students, or just the ones that were mentioned in the report?" Even if the schools in Washington DC are failing the students, there is no reason to believe that the majority of the 76 million plus students in our country are not being educated appropriately.

The saddest truth of this chapter in *Your First Year as a Principal* is that I feel I should inform you that even if you do report good news of your school to your local newspaper, there is a good chance the report will never see the headlines. While it might reach the fifth page, it most likely will be a small paragraph toward the bottom of the page that is almost impossible to notice. If you have a catastrophe or an incident, however, which is horrible news, it most likely will be the leading headline on the front page.

As stated, it is wise for you to know your school inside out, know the students by name, know their parents, know your staff, and remember to be prepared. If you are prepared you can look at being confronted by the media in a totally different perspective. You can consider using the media to your advantage in the event of a crisis. By working with the media you can tell the public exactly what the facts are, what they need to know, and the details that may help you in a mission to calm parents, students, staff, and the community. Consider that it is better the media come to you rather than taking statements from someone who does not know the whole story or has only second hand information. If these are the people the media is forced to contact, they will get false information, information that has been taken out of context, or information that is third or fourth hand, and is misleading.

If the time comes that you must speak to the media in reference to a crisis tell only the truth. Any lie you speak will catch up to you. If you don't know the answer to a question tell them you will get the answer and get back to them. Once you do find the answer, follow up and contact the media person that asked the question. It is important to always look a reporter in the eye. If you are being recorded do not look at the camera, and stay focused on the question at hand. Do not elaborate and do not get sidetracked. Sometimes it may seem the questions are harsh or accusatory, but it may be the shock and sensitivity you are feeling is due to the crisis and not necessarily any criticism on the part of the reporter. Regardless — always answer forthright and as though the question has been asked on a normal basis. It is important to speak of "the community" and to assure that the most important concern of the district is for the family, staff and students. Principal Barbara Belanger advises new principals to ..."be transparent. Never try to hide something because it will always come out that you were not truthful. Protecting your students has to be the first priority and when in doubt about answering to the media, get guidance from someone who has been there."

In our world today, especially in the aftermath of Columbine and the World Trade Center, it is not possible for a principal to honestly say, "Nothing will ever happen at my school." Even with the violent incidents that have taken place in schools throughout the world over the last 10 years, funding for safety precautions is practically nonexistent, minimal at best. Making a statement that there is not enough funding for security is not going to save you when a crisis takes place on your watch. You are going to be put under a microscope, scrutinized intensely, and possibly called on to testify in court. Being prepared is your only option.

Please do not despair just yet. Even with all this doom and gloom there is good news.

Think back to when you were attending college, then think of all you have heard from veteran principals on their experiences. There is no possible way college can prepare you for the job of school leader. Your job is unique in that it is one which requires on-job training, training that you can not learn anywhere else. There is no possible way a school can truly prepare you for every scenario you will face each day as a principal. There are no clear cut answers to the issues you will confront; therefore, while you are working you are learning to tackle any situation — good or bad. As a principal you will walk in the gray area throughout your career, never again having only black or white answers. The longer you work as a principal the better you will become at doing your job. The better your relationships will be with your school community, the better you will handle each incident as it occurs. To state it plainly: You, as a principal, will only be as good as your relationships are with your school community.

The better principal you are, the better you will handle any situation, and the more help you will have in doing so. If you are a good principal you will find your staff, students, and teachers behind you, all the way, while you are doing damage control. If you are not a worthwhile leader, you are going to find yourself standing on one side of the line all alone, regardless of why the line was drawn. Strive to be a good principal and take comfort in knowing you will not be alone in a time of crisis or in the aftermath.

Handling communications during a time of crisis is a gift that you, hopefully, will never need. It is good to know how to handle communications during a crisis just in case the necessity does ever occur. If you are fortunate enough to have a crisis management team, a crisis response is something that should be in place. It is the crisis management team's job to assist in support and information not only during, but also after, a distressing event.

Some schools have an individual who will be the "speaker" in times of distress. It is wonderful if you have someone who can do the job, but having a back-up is just as important. What if the crisis involves the speaker and he or she is unable to do the job of communicating with the community, parents, students, staff, and media? This is why a back-up is so important. Remember the objective of the crisis management team is to have a plan of action in the event of any crisis.

The importance of your crisis management team having regular meetings and updates can never be overstated. Simulation crisis plans should be practiced. Procedures should be observed and performed. Roles should be reviewed and periodically discussed. Your school should have an emergency evacuation site. This is where your students and staff will go in case they must be evacuated. Your procedures for a crisis should be written and distributed to all members of the team, and your teachers and staff need to know the plan thoroughly. Remember to have contact numbers for each member of the team, which should include home, school, work, cell, and beeper numbers.

If you play your cards right you can get an upper hand on handling the media before anything happens: have a good relationship with the reporter who will be responsible for news on your school. There is always a chance that nothing bad will ever happen at your educational establishment, but knowing the reporter at the local newspaper is still advisable. After making a phone call and scheduling an appointment, take a trip to meet the people of the local paper. With a copy of upcoming events in hand, go to the office and introduce yourself to the editor. Explain to him or her that you have school events you would like to submit, and if possible, you would like to meet the reporter who will be taking care of this information. Having a relationship with your newspaper's staff is a good move. It is important to learn about the paper's deadline. You don't want to submit information at a late hour if you wish to have it in the paper that day. Keep names, phone numbers, fax numbers, and addresses of the newspaper contacts on hand. Be sure to have a policy in your school stating who will be authorized to provide information and speak with the media. Many schools will have this policy in place, and you would do to find out if your district has such a policy, and to know exactly what that policy states.

Promoting your school is something that you may or may not be a natural in doing. It is in your best interest, and your schools', to invite the reporter to the school for a walk-through. This is a relaxing way to communicate with him or her on your turf, and at the same time give them a chance to become more comfortable with the school building, grounds, and more importantly, the atmosphere.

A word of advice is needed here. There are many wonderful things happening in schools all over the country every day. Even though the bashing of schools has become prominent in the media, the only way it can ever change is if we start spreading good news of what is going on inside the schools. Some would say educating a bunch of kids is rather boring and of no interest to the public, but if you look outside the box you may be surprised at all the interesting news taking place inside the walls of your educational establishment. There are special awards, presentations, seminars, school plays, artistic donations, community volunteerism, and many other wonderful incidents taking place every day. Share these occasions with the media. Let your community know their schools are not located on the fifth ring of hell where the children are beaten and enslaved by trolls. If you do not let them know, who will?

It is advisable that you take Principal Fielding's advice on public relations: "…be proactive in getting out the good news."

Another word of advice seems needed before we are off and running into a new area of being a first-year principal. "Off the record," is not necessarily a safe-guard at any time, regardless of your relationship with news people. Always remember that just because a reporter agrees you can speak "off the record," it does not mean what you say will not be reported. If you are lucky enough to know a reporter personally, and you are good friends with this person, you may speak off the record if you wish. Otherwise, it probably is not worth taking the chance. Principal Pichard advises first-year principals to "be careful of the press. What you say may not be what is printed. Always use your Public Relations Department, if the school district has a contact, to bounce things off it before sending any items or talking about sensitive issues."

How Important are You?

According to the Southern Regional Education Board (SREB) you are extremely important. SREB, an Atlanta based policy group whose mission is to "help states achieve the *12 Challenge to Lead Goals for Education*," reports there are many prospective principals with the proper educational credentials, but few who are capable of being good school leaders. The shortage of these potential leaders is "crucial," according to SREB. The group states the role of principals in improving schools and increasing student achievement is also crucial. They have identified 13 critical success factors that are associated with principals who have improved student achievement in their schools. These factors are:

- Focusing on student achievement

- Developing a culture of high expectations

- Designing a standards-based instructional system

- Creating a caring environment

- Implementing data-based improvement

- Communicating

- Involving parents

- Initiating and managing change

- Providing professional development

- Innovating

- Maximizing resources

- Building external support

- Staying abreast of effective practices.

Also according to SREB, when considering the characteristics of a good school principal one must look for the following:

- One who can make constructive and beneficial decisions for students, staff, teachers, parents, community, and the establishment as a whole.

- One with motivation and determination.

- One who has good leadership and supervisory skills.

- One who can communicate effectively.

- One with knowledge in educational practices.

- One who is computer savvy.

How important are you? It is believed that the principal is the responsible party for setting the atmosphere for the entire school. If you are a weak leader you will not be viewed as a leader at all, merely a figurehead, a puppet run by a strong-willed teacher or an overbearing superintendent who happens to be a bully. If you are a strong leader, you will be followed, not fallowed.

The opposite side of the spectrum is looking at the effects of a bad principal. A bad principal can ruin a good school in as little as a few weeks. Bringing around a troubled and failing school may take more time, but a good principal can certainly achieve that attainable and worthwhile goal. Good principals are a draw for good teachers. Bad principals chase away good teachers.

A good principal needs to know how students learn and how teachers teach. By knowing these two important elements you are already halfway to the goal of becoming a good leader. This knowledge will help you when choosing new curriculums and resources for your teachers. Not only does a great leader know these two basics thoroughly, he or she knows the necessity of caring about the individual students and staff, and the school community as a whole.

If you, as a principal, understand how students are learning, and how your students learn best, you already have a deep understanding of your student body. If you, as a principal, understand how your teachers need to constantly improve their own skills, you already have set a goal for them to meet, a goal which will help your students, staff and school community become successful.

What your state, school board and community expect of their school leaders is more or less what they expect of their students. If your state does not care what kind of school leaders they have, they do not put much emphasis on education for students. If your school board looks for a principal with a doctorate but does not put any emphasis on how the candidate for principal feels about children, they most likely are going to get a bad principal.

Basically — it all comes down to you. When things go good for your school community it most likely will be the school board and the superintendent who get the credit. When things go bad, you will get the blame. You are responsible for what happens in your school, the outcome of your student's education, whether or not you have good or bad teachers, how well or poorly they teach, and the success or failure of your students as future citizens. In looking over this partial list, it is easy to see why you are crucial to the position of principal.

In today's schools you will be faced with solving problems constantly, scrutinizing troubles that are complex, using your knowledge and skills to improve learning, and showing leadership qualities on a daily basis. It will be up to you to set the pace of learning, advancing, and achieving for your students and teachers.

Although you will take the fall alone if there is a catastrophe or incident in your school, you need a team to accomplish your goals. Any principal who acts alone will find him or her self alone, riding a high but quickly descending to failure. By having a team you are implementing changes, changes that you know are needed. The team helps you by being on the same page, and having the same mission and goals. When there is a team the group becomes larger simply because people see others believing in something; they ascertain it is a mission worth believing in. A principal is the leader of the team; another way in which you are important.

When asked good principals admit they are responsible for their school, and all who attend it, but if it is one which is recognized as an excellent school, or if it is one that has been turned around, they will be the first to tell you that they did not do it alone. When great principals work with a team of teachers from their schools, they are helping to groom leaders for the future. Imagine going to a meeting or seminar with a group of teachers. What will happen after the meeting, during the ride home? They will converse with one another about the speaker and toss ideas around. This is putting your team on the same page, creating a unified vision, enhancing relationships, delegating responsibility, and training teachers to become future school leaders.

All excellent principals have the knowledge and skills to improve student achievement by improving curriculums and instruction. Great principals improve morale, give attention to individuals, and give special attention where needed. Great principals lead by example, and drive a school community toward success.

Giving up power is difficult for some people. If you wishes to have a good team you will need to give up some of your authority. Delegating responsibility means allowing others to take charge of a certain functions. You are still responsible, but if you are wise you will share that responsibility and give yourself a break, as well as giving someone else a chance to lead in an area where they fit best.

A good synonym for "most important" is principal. The two are perfectly tied, and it is an ideal example for acknowledging how crucial a good principal is. Some other synonyms for "most important" are vital, essential, crucial, primary, and leading. This is being brought to your attention to verify that a principal is named such because a principal is the most important administrator in school leadership.

As a dedicated leader you are the one the school community will turn to. You are the one who makes the decisions, implements the changes, encourages and listens to others, assembles, improves, and rewards. You are expected to be the one who will stand beside your staff and students when they need you. To be a leader you must influence the motivations and goals of others. You are the balance between management and leadership activities. You are the one that holds everything together.

Some states are looking at a critical shortage of good leadership applicants. In 1993 Michigan had half as many more applicants looking to become principals than what they have today. Florida was in a crucial state of affairs because the majority of their principals were about to retire. They made an offer to the principals and were blessed with the many agreeing to stay and work with candidates who wished to become principals.

Exactly what makes a "qualified" principal? According to a personnel director in Michigan, it takes seven years to become a competent teacher, but the candidates applying for position of principal had only three years of teaching experience. With a large number of principals retiring, and the shortage of qualified candidates, some states are concerned about what will happen to their schools in the future. Additional burdens make the role of principal less desirable explaining why there are fewer applicants, but less qualified applicants are a mystery. Some believe that teachers are more satisfied in their positions today than before; better pay and retirement, and more resources. Still good principals are getting harder to find which means the students will have a harder time learning in quality schools.

Your position as principal is important to hundreds of students as well as teachers, parents, school administration personnel, and communities. Without good leaders our schools will graduate under-educated adults; the students will not become productive citizens.

There have been articles written in which principals are compared to Wonder Woman or Superman, and with the endless job requirements it is not surprising. Many communities have become aware of the principals' growing responsibilities. They have hired assistant principals and administrative assistants. Just as we previously mentioned, teaching the same curriculums across the nation would still be problematic due to the individuality of each teacher. Having the principals' responsibilities delegated would have to be different in each school as well. Principals also are individuals and the responsibilities they would be willing to delegate would depend on each principal's preference. One principal might enjoy public relations where another would prefer choosing and placing curriculum.

The question of which responsibility principals enjoy most was surprising: student discipline. It seems the greatest leaders enjoy the personal contact with their students, and helping them make good choices. Giving reinforcement and being a patient guide for students to become good citizens is most important to good leaders. Many principals also say that spending time with their students, even in the matter of discipline, is how they know what is really happening in their schools. One principal said he has a way of talking to students when they are in trouble so that they want to do better, and he takes the time to check on them periodically so they know he cares.

The three items that top the list as duties principals do not like to deal with are upset parents, budgeting, and teacher evaluations. Budgeting is very time-consuming, evaluation instruments never work to improve teaching or learning, and non-supportive parents are annoying on a daily, or almost daily basis.

In today's society the schools are always being second-guessed. Schools have been put in a defensive position. Parents have diverse expectations. States tell schools what to do or not do without any input from school personnel. Students are on their own and raise themselves. They learn respect only at the school. Communities give tax breaks to businesses just to get them in the city limits eliminating money that goes to the schools. These issues and more are reasons there are fewer qualified candidates applying for principals' jobs. Yet here you are a first-year principal about to embark on a ride you will never forget.

All this and more is why you, as a first-year principal, must take into consideration yourself as a person, not just a principal.

> *"As a principal your work is never done, but you have to make the decision that enough is enough, and that sometimes you need time for yourself...I know this is a problem for, especially, new principals."*
>
> **Barbara Belanger**
> Harbor City Elementary
> Melbourne, Florida

Taking Care of You

Since the traditional expectations of principals remain, and more have been added to the list, burn-out has become the concern for our school leaders. With 12 to 15 hour days being the norm, evening activities you must attend, meetings you must schedule, state mandates you must follow to the letter, teachers to evaluate, research to analyze and implement, seminars to attend, parents to meet, students to discipline, and the numerous other tasks you must perform, many would ask why anyone would want the principal's job? Still — there are those of you who do. In order to be successful you must remember one important ingredient in the mixture of leadership: taking care of yourself.

My grandmother who is 93 years old, and not only southern but stubborn as hell, once made a statement in regard to my being a mother of four, and the statement has stayed with me ever since. She said, "Why, Tena, if you don't take care of yourself, how on earth are you going to be able to take care of all those kids?" This is advice you would do well to heed. If you do not take care of yourself, how on earth are you going to take care of all those students who depend on your being there for them?

You were most likely a teacher before you became a principal. If this is the case you have found yourself on a different playing field than where you once were. You are no longer a teacher, and you will not be treated as one of the group. It is not so much that you are no longer liked or appreciated; it is more that you are no longer one of them. You are now an administrative figure, the authoritarian, and let us face the truth: you are the one who can have them fired.

There will be times of loneliness in this job principal. Leaders are not one of the gang but rather an entity all on their own. You do not belong with the superintendent or the teachers, so where do you belong? It is unfortunate in that you are on your own. You would do well to find other principals you can talk to. There are many services in numerous states where they now have mentoring programs for principals. Check to see if your state offers one. Some states make it mandatory for first-year principals to attend these programs before becoming a principal because they know how isolated a principal can feel.

Not only will you feel a time of loneliness once you are performing this job, you will also feel sadness. You are giving up a position you knew and were comfortable in. Now you have taken on something that is bigger than you expected and you may be uncomfortable as an authority figure. This is to be expected so take heart. It is perfectly normal for those who make a life change, and leave something familiar behind, to feel nostalgic for a while. It is much like leaving a part of yourself behind, and moving into an area in which you are unfamiliar.

You might take the position as principal at the school where you taught. If so, you may expect everything to remain the same. But some of the principals who have done this stated that "it was not a good move."

Not only were they surrounded by teachers with whom they once had camaraderie, but there were those who shunned them. Such behavior could be explained as jealousy, envy, a sense of betrayal, or possibly even anger. It is possible that some of the teachers would attempt to take advantage of your past friendship and new position by coming to you with complaints and expecting favorable action. There might even come a time when you enter the teachers' lounge and all conversations stop. You could find yourself standing in a room full of people, the silence almost tangible in its thickness, the room reeking of disapproval. This kind of reaction would hurt your feelings and make you feel awkward, lonely and isolated. Take heart that in time, things would even out and your position would become defined and your leadership appreciated by most, if not all, your teachers. However, you could not expect to ever be "one of the gang" again. You would be their leader, not one of the brigade members.

You must take time for your family and friends, and for yourself. You will find this is not so easy to do. You rose from bed with the alarm at 5:30 a.m. and arrived at work by 6:45. You have been on the move all day, and finally, the dismissal bell rings. You stand at the door and say "goodbye" to the students and teachers, then go to your office to take care of some paperwork. You enter your room to find the pile of papers has somehow grown, and the one-inch thick stack is now four inches high. There are post-it notes with messages from callers who wish to speak with you, the small yellow squares having taken over your desk while you were out. You take a deep breath, and start going through the mound of papers, placing them in order according to priority. With the pile now in order you go through the yellow sticky notes, placing them in a line, most important first, and so on. You hear the last bus pull out of the parking lot, and start making phone calls knowing it will take at least two hours. That still leaves the pile of paperwork you must finish, and the night grows longer.

Some people have a tendency to refuse to quit until the job is finished.

This can be a wonderful quality or a horrid curse. As a principal you must constantly remind yourself that your job is never done. You must force yourself to say, enough, and pack it in for the night. If you do not follow this self-inflicted rule, you will never see your family. If you do not follow this rule, you will burn out within three years, and never be the wonderful leader you have the potential to be.

You will find that your role in friendships will change. You may feel like you are the same person, but you will not be viewed the same by others. We have discussed how your position will change your status with the teachers, but you must expect it to change with some of your personal friendships as well. You may find some friends simply disappear or do not return your calls. It is not easy to understand, but there are those who will feel you are on a different level with your new position; they are uncomfortable with this change in the playing field. There are those who will feel you no longer play on the same playground as they do, that you have moved on to a new and different playground, leaving them behind in the same place they have always been. While this is not how you feel or view your new status in life, it may be how others will view it. You are now viewed in a different light — like it or not.

Your family may have thought they knew what to expect with your new role as principal. Suddenly you find your spouse upset that you are getting home at 8 p.m. rather than the usual 3:30 or 4 o'clock. Now your spouse is upset because you missed dinner again, and the kids had to go to bed without your saying good night. Rather than become estranged with your family, force yourself to stick with that self-inflicted rule and say, enough is enough. No, you will not get all the paperwork finished. You may not get all the calls answered either, but you will have some time with your family, and that is a priority you must keep in mind. If for no other reason, walk away at a certain hour because the truth is the paperwork will never be finished and all the phone calls will never be answered on the day the calls were made. There always will be paperwork to do and calls to answer, but your children will not be young forever, and your spouse may not be able to deal with your never being part of the family.

There is support out there for first-year principals. Not only will you find someone in your building who will become your comrade, but most likely, you will find best friends within the first year of your new position. Your secretary may become your confidante. Or it may be one of the teachers, or even the custodian. Regardless, you will find the person you can confide in, relate your troubles to, or simply vent frustrations to. Whoever this person is, they will always be there, taking time to listen and never saying a word to the rest of the staff about your troubles and worries. It may be a principal in another school that engages your friendship, but most likely, there will be someone in your educational establishment that will become your shoulder, just as you are a shoulder for so many others. Give it time, do not despair, and keep in mind that all will be well with time and patience.

Speaking of confidants, there are other principals out there that have the same need as you. Almost everyone needs someone to talk to, and other principals have the same needs, someone that understands their problems. No one understands your position as well as other principals, so it is advisable that this is where you should turn. According to Bill Hall, Director of Educational Leadership and Educational Development in Florida's Brevard School District, "mentors are self-selected." He says, "Each principal-preparer picks their own mentor for various and personal reasons." By allowing each principal-preparer the freedom to choose their own mentor, it takes some of the responsibility off the program director. More importantly the choice ascertains principal candidates they are getting a mentor they think they will be comfortable confiding in.

To be uncomfortable in your new position is perfectly normal; do not give up in the first or second year. You will not be giving yourself or the school a fair chance if you do. Take at least 3 to 5 years, allowing yourself time to adjust and learn how to manage, before deciding whether the position is one you are not going to be happy with. You will feel overwhelmed when you first step into the shoes of school leader; finding that your time is no longer your own, but everyone else's. You will never please everyone in this job at first, and that is not an easy fact to accept. However, it can be done in time, once you have learned to adjust and accept that you are only one person, one leader, and a one-man-show for an audience of thousands. Keep in mind that as long as people are talking about what you are doing, they are thinking, watching, and learning. Think about it — having your staff learn your vision and goals is exactly what you want them to do. So let them talk. Let them wonder and learn. This is a good thing, and that is what you need to keep in mind.

Most likely you will be tempted to quit, the overwhelming feeling of loneliness almost more than you can bear. Keep in mind that this feeling will pass in time, and it will only be a matter of months before your staff is welcoming a leader with passion, patience, caring, vision, and goals.

Know Your Limits

Everyone is an individual. Each person deals with stress in a different manner. Some people thrive on stressful situations, becoming more productive when their back is against the wall; others cave under the pressure. It is the same in all walks of life: some writers do a better job when they are up against a deadline while others fall apart and get writer's block. A production worker may be able to produce more parts, and meet their quota when they have only two hours of their shift left, while others will drop each piece, and falter under the pressure. You need to be aware of your personal limits, and adjust your schedule and workload accordingly. If an 8 hour day is all you can handle at the office, delegate some of the work and go home after 8 hours. You can always take paperwork home with you and delve into it after you relax and have dinner.

Too much stress will eventually put you in a place where you are working under emotional duress. Emotional duress is not a good place to be, especially when dealing with an assortment of people, conflict, or discipline. It would be fine if you could lock yourself in the office and stay there until you were re-energized and ready to face another 5 or 6 hours of constant demands. This is not a liberty you have; you will not be able to do the hide. You must deal with each incident as it occurs, or on some days, deal with each incident by priority.

There are many issues that trigger stress, just as there are many factors that will determine how you deal with the daily and constant stresses of your position. Self esteem, personal problems, whether you have a controlling personality, character traits, whether you are a perfectionist, and your gender are some of the traits that determine how you handle stress. Any of these behaviors will determine how you will deal with the stress of being an educational leader.

"Principals" and "stress" are synonymous in describing today's educational realm. It was reported on AM, a radio station in Australia, that the Victoria region was calling for a major review of school principals and their roles. The statewide study was done over a period of time, and a report made by the Victorian Education Department Commission, found nearly half the principals reported stress-related illnesses such as heart problems and severe headaches. The study also found that principals had suffered from breakdowns or even committed suicide. Due to the revealing evidence of this study, the Australian government stated it was time to support the principals and give them more resources.

Lynette J. Fields of the University of South Florida did a study on patterns of stress and coping mechanisms of school administrators. In her report it was stated that first-year principals and first-year assistant principals were most stressed by uncontrollable demands on their time, time taken away from their personal lives, prospective staffs, and conflict. The biggest stress relievers the principals and assistant principals were quoted to use were a sense of humor, exercise, and venting.

A sense of humor can get you through some extremely rough days. In Fields' study on first-year's and assistants, over 53% of first-year principals said they had found a sense of humor the perfect mechanism to get them through their first year on the job. Some first-year principals and their assistants found they could vent to one another and the understanding between the two make this a perfect union of friendship and understanding. Other first-year principals admitted to playing practical jokes on their assistants, finding a humorous way to get through the day. "Positive reinforcement" was another release mechanism found by a first-year principal who decided to initiate a talent show in her middle school. Unlike most talent shows that take place in schools, it was the teachers who did the skits. They made them humorous but educational. The students loved seeing their teachers, especially the tough ones, cutting up and having fun, and the teachers had a good time coming up with the ideas, and putting on a show for the kids.

A study in New Zealand found that 43% of their principals reported that stress levels over the previous week had been high or extremely high. The principals who reported being stressed were also high on the list for having illnesses, depression, anger, frustration, and little to poor sleep. The high or extremely high stress levels were reported to be related to job satisfaction.

It is important that you know yourself, your reactions to certain aspects of your job, your ability to handle those aspects, and which of those aspects has the worst affect on you mentally, physically, and emotionally. It is advisable to keep a journal, noting what happens on each day, when you are feeling stressed, and what takes place that causes the stress. Once you see which tasks or conflicts cause you to become the most anxious or tense, you can begin looking for someone on your staff that can take over those particular responsibilities.

As stated, burn-out of principals is a concern, and learning how to manage your stress can be beneficial to you, your staff, your students, your friends, and your family. Some possible positive outlets could be, getting away for a short weekend, reducing the number of events you attend, staying organized, not getting to far ahead of yourself, and taking one step at a time. Delegating jobs, having a confidante that you can vent to, understanding that most people who are angry are not angry at you but at something or someone else, and not falling into the habit of procrastinating are other ways to keep the stress level at a minimum.

On **www.EducationWorld.com** you can find an article with 30 suggestions for principals dealing with stress, and laughter is the first suggestion listed. Another proposal is for principals to keep a praise file. Any compliment from a teacher, student, administrator, or parent, any notes of praise written to you, should be kept in this file for future reference. It is advisable to pull out the file when you're feeling down or depressed because, in time, the number of notes will surprise you, and they will also remind you that the good outweighs the bad. Read, surf the net, listen to music, spend time with the students, and do other activities are some of the other suggestions found on Education World. More suggestions that can help you deal with stress include enjoying nature, planning or cooking a meal, spending time with your pet, working in the garden, planning your time, doing things with friends outside of school, watching a favorite television show, and taking a weekend off.

The coming crisis, having too few qualified principals, is being felt in Australia as well as in the United States. In a Federal Government report by the Australian Council for Education Research, it was stated that there were not enough applicants for becoming a principal due to stress and time demands of the job. Government educational departments all over the world are discovering that school leadership has an impact on learning, and with that knowledge as well as the shortage of upcoming principals, their attention has been peaked. With the role of school principal having drastically changed over the past 10 years and the demands on school principals having become almost humanly impossible, people in high places are starting to notice. Once it was determined that students learn more and better with a great leader, school principals and the demanding tasks placed on them, began getting some attention. We are talking about government, however, so it will take time before anything is changed for the better. On a good note, now you know there are things you can do to make your position easier, and there are several states implementing mentor and leadership programs to help you.

If you are a natural worrier, by all means, learn how to change that personality trait. Demands on principals are high enough without worrying needlessly. Worry causes health problems, raises stress levels, and can turn you into a hateful or depressed person when you normally are not. Do not waste valuable energy on trivial matters or issues that you have no control over. Make a list of the issues that you tend to worry about, then go back and look at them a few days later. Think about these issues, whether you have any control, and realize where you are wasting your strength, time and energy.

Be proactive in taking care of yourself. Keep in mind the wise words of my 93-year-old grandmother in regards of taking care of yourself so you can care for others. Play, laugh, and have fun. Just because you are an adult does not mean you are no longer allowed to play.

In the words of the Naples, Florida, Estates Elementary School Principal, Olliver Phipps, "Have fun. You have to have fun or you'll burn out on this job. Whatever it takes to make it fun, do it, even if it's just sitting on the floor laughing with the kindergartners. If that is fun for you, then do it. Do it every day if that is what you need."

7
END RESULT

———

To achieve and maintain a high level of leadership that is learning-centered, school principals must have support. This support must come from the school system, university, and state education leaders. These leaders must also have a good understanding of the present and future demands on every school and classroom. They must understand these demands to offer present and future leaders what is needed. Exactly what is needed?

When discussing how the role of principal has changed, Bill Hall, Director of the Leadership and Professional Development Department for Brevard Public Schools in Florida said, "Leadership has changed by light-years — tenfold. I equate the change to The Gulf, from hickory shaft to graphite." The demands are endless, the time precious little, the importance of doing the job right, imperative. What is the future outlook for principals? Bill Hall said, "Principals and assistant principals cannot do it anymore. They need help. With accountability, legislation, social problems...one has to distribute accountability. The changes that must be made are in resourcefulness, time management, and money. There are always huge budget cuts, now on a large scale like never seen before. Next year Brevard will lose 20 to 30 million dollars. Orange County will lose 70 million dollars. There has to be more resourcefulness."

With jobs leaving the country tax dollars are shrinking at a rapid pace. This means more budget cuts in education, leaving principals and superintendents on their own to find resources for their staff and schools. There are already thousands of teachers balking at the amount of money they must spend out of their own pockets to have supplies for their students, and there are more cuts to come. If the teachers cannot afford to use their own money, the principals have no funding for purchasing supplies or resources for their teachers. Where will this leave the education of our children?

Another area of concern for future school leaders is ethics. "Brevard is very successful on programs for our school leaders, but in the future I see us having to look at how to model ethical leadership. There are too many instances of illegal and unethical activities in the schools of America today, such as sexual abuse. There are good people out there making stupid mistakes," said Hall.

The demands are endless and there seems to be no limit in site for the demands that are to come. What is the future outlook for principals? How does a first-year principal make the most of his leadership today and for years to come? The best way to attain success is to look where success is being achieved.

Measuring Success

Let us look at some successful schools in hope that you will find out what works. After viewing the facts about these excellent schools perhaps you can look at your own school with a different perspective to see where things could possibly improve. Or maybe you can garner a few ideas to continue the road to success that your school is already traveling.

It should not be necessary to say, but once you take your position, if there are increases in complaints, students being moved to different schools, a decline in student performance and achievement, or staff taking jobs in a different school, there is obviously a problem with your leadership. If your students are not learning, this is a measurement of your effectiveness as a school leader.

If, by chance, this is the situation you find yourself in, you need to question whether you have chosen the right fire. If you still feel that being a school leader is what you wish to do, find someone who can give you feedback on how you are doing as a leader. This person must be someone who is honest and not afraid of telling you the truth. That is the only way you will discover what you may or may not be doing wrong. It is suggested that if you do not have a mentor, you need to find one. Having a mentor is an invaluable resource in helping improve your skills, provide a lifeline when needed, and maintaining you sanity when it is threatened.

Let us look at some of the schools, and school leaders, that are succeeding, so that we may discover where they are different from schools and school leaders that are failing.

A study in Canadian education reported the Edmonton Catholic Schools held the best practices in education, and excellence in student achievement. When glancing through the Web site of the Edmonton Catholic Schools, it is easy to see why they have been reported as a school of excellence. They offer numerous programs for students, staff, and parents. One of their claims to excellence is that "teachers and principals take pride in our district because they share in the planning, decision making and student successes." In Alberta there is an "Accountability Pillar Report" that is a measure established by Alberta Education which gives all school boards in Alberta a consistent way to measure how well learning goals are achieved.

The Good Shepherd Catholic School in Santa Cruz, California, has a parent club. Their Web site states that all parents are members of the parent club. The principal of Good Shepherd, David Sullivan, trained for principal through the ACE Leadership Program at Notre Dame. Sullivan says, "There is a growing absence of leadership in schools everywhere." Staff of Good Shepherd says it is common to find Sullivan on the playground with the students during recess and lunch, taking part in their activities. It is said that Sullivan is a man who promotes the virtues of the community.

Dr. Cassandra Hopkins is principal at River's Edge Elementary School in Georgia. Dr. Hopkins' mission is to educate students "through respect for self and others, expectations of excellence, envisioning the future, and superior education in a safe environment." Hopkins also states that the school staff and leader cannot be successful in their mission without the parents' assistance, "for successful parental involvement nurtures relationships and fosters partnerships." It is Hopkins' belief that it takes teachers, teacher assistants, administrators, and parents working together to produce children who are confident and lifelong learners. Hopkins also has a "my door is always open" policy.

In Boston, Massachusetts, Superintendent Dr. Thomas Payzant took on Boston Public Schools, a district with over 58,000 students, 4,700 teachers, and a district where 73 percent of the children live in poverty. Payzant attacked the problems head-on in the Boston Public Schools, and shepherded a set of ongoing reforms called Focus on Children because he believes "American education will never improve for students if it's taken one school at a time." He stated that one of the most critical goals was refining strong school principals. Within Payzant's first year he created a leadership team and has since established the Boston School Leadership Institute.

After dramatic gains in student achievement in 2005-2006, twenty-four schools in the Plano, Texas, Independent School District (ISD) won the prestigious honor, the National Blue Ribbon School of Excellence. In the Plano School District mission and goals statement it reads they "believe Public education is the foundation of our democratic principles and is our best economic investment." The goals and mission statement also states that "successful learning is best achieved through strong connections with parents, families and all sectors of the broader community." The Web site for the ISD Plano School District is set up for easy access by parents, students, and staff as well as others in the community. The Superintendent of the ISD Plano School District, Dr. Doug Otto, won the "21 Leaders for the 21st century" award. Dr. Otto is known as "one of the nation's leaders in educational technology, school administration, and school finance." Plano ISD's awards and honors are vast, their mission to "ensure that all students are provided with an excellent education," is one they have achieved.

For schools that have more than "42.5 percent of the students living in non-English homes, where English is not the first language and sometimes isn't spoken," Collier County Public Schools in Florida have met this challenge head-on. There are more than 6,000 students in their English for Speakers of Other Languages (ESOL) program. The percentage of non-English homes rises "to 49.3 percent in grades Pre-K through grade 3, where learning to read is critical. Approximately 45.2 percent of the student population is categorized as economically needy and qualify for free or reduced lunch." With diversity of students ranging from White, Black, Hispanic, Haitian, Mixed, Asian, and Indian, the teachers, principals, school board, and superintendent have their hands full. Finding the means to communicate and then teach is a constant concern. Collier County has had the ESOL Program since 1984 when they had a "total of 250 students enrolled. In 2007 the ESOL Program had a total enrollment of 6,388 students," of which 4,203 of them were in the elementary level. "Collier County's Public Schools ESOL students speak 81 different heritage languages, and come from 147 different countries of origin." Even with so much diversity Collier County Public Schools has a current graduation rate of 74.7 percent and a current dropout rate of 2.0 percent. The state grades the schools on an A+ Plan, and 20 of the 44 Collier schools received an A at the end of the 2006-2007 school year; six received a B. The District School Board states that their number one shared belief is "students are our number one priority and their needs are the focus of all district decisions."

We have looked at six schools of excellence, all focused on giving their students the best education possible, all having exceptional leaders with vision and goals, and the best leaders have quality staff that share their vision and goals. Now let us look at one more school district, one that affected the end result for *Your First Year as a Principle*: Florida's Brevard School District.

In my cyber travels for research I was fortunate in finding Dr. Eric J. Smith, the Commissioner of the Florida Department of Education. Dr. Smith turned me over to Superintendent Dr. Richard A. DiPatri, who was enthusiastic about the idea of having his principals take part in helping with my project, *Your First Year as a Principal*. After all Brevard Public Schools received the 2007 Governor's Sterling Award for being a role model for excellence in organizational performance. Brevard District is only the second school district in Florida to receive this prestigious recognition.

Dr. DiPatri oversees the very diversified and distinguished Brevard Public Schools; there are 126 in all. In these educational establishments there are more than 74,000 students ranging from Pre-Kindergarten through 12th grade. Of the 74 thousand plus students there are more than 12,000 who fall into the range preset by Individual Handicap Disabled. Over 1,500 students of Brevard Schools' primary language is other than English. In 2005-2006, Brevard Schools had a graduation ratio of 90.7 percent and a drop-out rate of 0.8 percent.

With the excessive number of students, the diversity of these students, the range of ages and disabilities of the Exceptional Students, and the challenge of having students who have limited English, Dr. DiPatri has every reason to be proud of his staff and student body.

The key to running a successful school lies in Dr. DiPatri's sincere words, "We work together as a team." Another team player in the Brevard School District led me through the overwhelming information on the school district's Web site. This team player is Bill Hall, Director of the Educational Leadership and Professional Development Department. When asked what Brevard's secret for success is, Hall responded, "Our secret is the leadership of the district. There is one man who is responsible for all of it, one individual with vision and focus that he passes on, and that is Dr. DiPatri."

Named Superintendent of the Year by the Florida Association of District School Superintendents, DiPatri leads by example. DiPatri has been called a "power-hitter," and a "visionary instructional leader." One board member credited DiPatri with having "laser-like focus on student achievement." DiPatri said that, "one of the most satisfying aspects of his job was developing school principals into instructional leaders."

Prior to becoming superintendent of Brevard County School District, DiPatri served in New Jersey as a teacher, coordinator, principal, superintendent of schools, Special Assistant to the Commissioner of Education, and State District Superintendent of Schools.

In reading over the monthly newsletters Dr. DiPatri has written, it is easy to see why he is such a well-known leader, an exemplary role model, and a good man. One newsletter headlined, "In Brevard Public Schools, the People Make the Difference." When DiPatri says, "the people," he means all the people. He is a strong believer in everyone being a part of each student's education. "The people who work on that team — from teachers and administrators to bus drivers and cafeteria workers — come to work every day ready to foster a positive environment for student achievement," says DiPatri.

As an exceptional leader, DiPatri never forgets that teaching students education and citizenship is attained through the team that is working together. Another newsletter written by DiPatri reads, "Thanks to the strong support of our School Board, the hard work of our teachers, staff, administrators and district personnel, and the proactive involvement of our parents, we are laying the foundation for new levels of student achievement."

When looking at the Web site of the Brevard County School District one becomes amazed when realization sinks in. The vast amount of educational programs offered to the employees of the Brevard District is phenomenal. There are programs for everyone — instructional and non-instructional employees alike. If anyone in the system wishes to educate and better themselves, DiPatri and Hall are sure to offer the opportunity to do so. What better way is there to lead than doing so by example?

In Dr. DiPatri's September 2007 newsletter he wrote, "These days it is common knowledge that students whose parents are actively involved and concerned about their educational progress tend to have higher levels of achievement. Still, it never hurts to remind parents that the more engaged they are in their children's growth and development, the better chances they have of positively influencing their maturation into educated, contributing members of society." DiPatri went on to write, "One hundred percent of the research studies upon which the campaign is based, compiled by The

Parent Institute, indicate that parent involvement has a significant impact on student success." The campaign DiPatri is referring to is the Be There parent campaign at Brevard County Schools. "Be There" was started in Volusia County after it was "agreed that parents play a critical role in the success of children and schools." Brevard Schools started their "Be There" campaign in the fall of the 2007-2008 school year.

The newsletter of September of 2006 was written in regards to safety. In the newsletter Dr. DiPatri asked for the parents to help in keeping the children safe, writing that it "is all our responsibility — students, parents, teachers and administrators — to be sure we are doing everything we can to keep our children safe and secure."

As a man of vision, DiPatri was aware of a problem looming on the horizon, that of losing many seasoned principals as they approached retirement. Brevard was looking at losing as many as15 principals at one time. DiPatri created a goal of preparing the district for the wave of retirements, unwilling to lose the massive experience these leaders would be taking with them. This was the start of his succession plan — the mentoring and training of future leaders. The amazing part of this plan is that it has evolved, and is no longer just for principals, but for everyone "from cafeteria managers and childcare coordinators to ground supervisors and head custodians."

To be able to look far enough ahead, DiPatri has saved Brevard County Schools what could have been a disaster. Losing many wise leaders at one time could have sent their students into a tail-spin. DiPatri knew that, and took the matter seriously. With the help of Bill Hall, another great man of vision and heart, they prepared for the loss of their leaders by having those leaders mentor and train new blood. This program is not a new idea, but was handled by two men who were willing to put in long hours and heartfelt caring to pull it off, and then take it further than most have ever considered.

Leadership and Mentoring

The idea behind the leadership and mentoring programs at Brevard Schools is to continue the direction in which the school has been going under the present leader. The reason this is important is that "Established learning communities are more likely to be disrupted or discontinued when a new leader steps into the principalship. Internal focus on the leadership sustainability can certainly counter this discontinuity of direction," explains Hall. It has been proven that when a new principal steps into the position of leader, if this leader is not open-minded and thoughtful in his steps to take the predecessor's place, the whole school community can be thrown into chaos and failure. Hall explains, "The continuity of direction that results from internal leadership development can preserve the core of a school or district's culture and allow it to stand strong against the buffeting winds of change despite new leaders taking over the helm. Schools and districts that do not put into place processes and structures that allow them to stay the course amidst changes in the individual leader are more likely to expose themselves to external change agents who could dismantle what is current practice. Internal leadership development can inoculate these organizations against any possible attack on their culture."

When Hall was asked how Brevard was going to handle losing 15 valuable leaders in the near future he enthusiastically stated, "By using the senior staff, having the formal succession plan, leadership development, and by having the entire organization be a part of the succession plan. It is all about putting the process in place so everyone can be replaced with someone new and still have a high performing school district."

Hall said that most districts "focus just on senior leadership," but he believes in "building talent from within. Brevard has what they call the job family. That is, we look within the family, look at their skills and map out a development plan with that in mind."

Knowing they had an oncoming disaster with the retirement of 15 valued leaders, Brevard called in a consulting firm — "because we had no model to go by" — said Hall. Instead of violating development "we talked about succession planning and learned of a group out of Boca Raton," contacted them and spent over a year working on reports, ideas, and a solid plan based on best practice". The plan the consulting firm handed over was, "huge," said Hall. "It would have taken massive time, a complete overhaul, rethinking of philosophy... Instead, we decided to work with Human Resources and used feedback. We were still able to do our jobs. We decided to take on what we could do that made sense, and was doable, and roll out what we could, and put the plan in place."

"It is a roadmap," explained Hall of the leadership and mentoring program. "Working with the consulting firm added credibility to what we did." According to Hall, their ideas were fantastic, but not doable. The plan the district came up with instead was the one that worked. Not only has it worked, but it has led to other great plans that are being put into place.

The idea of the leadership program, how it "prepares successors from cafeteria managers and childcare coordinators to ground supervisors and head custodians" is Hall's vision. "It's what I think about at night instead of sleeping."

Hall believes that, "Instructional leaders have a moral obligation to ensure that our schools contribute to the sustainability of leadership in the profession. The best vehicle to carry out this moral imperative exists in the constructs of professional learning communities. We are morally obligated to pass the torch of leadership that was once passed to us. When you pass the torch of leadership, first make sure it's lit."

I asked Hall how long the leadership program had been in place at Brevard. He explained that the state had put management training in place in the late 1970's, early 1980's. The state provided funds, and set up five regional programs. "This is what I grew up with," said Hall, who has been with Brevard Schools for 39 years, 16 as Director of Leadership and Professional Development. "The training the state offered was free, but they did away with it. We have tried to develop what we are doing through the idea of that program."

Hall believes there are six essential strategies to promote leadership sustainability.

- Create a formal leadership development plan.

- Develop a succession plan with a management component.

- Create a framework that provides for lateral and vertical capacity building.

- Develop collaborative leadership team/guiding coalitions which support and promote distributed accountability.

- Put teachers into collaborative teams/professional learning communities(PLCs) and appoint one teacher as leader of each team.

- Make leadership development a specific essential job function on all administrative/supervisory job descriptions.

The leadership and mentoring program in Brevard County has their candidates in training "before leadership." They are certified for two years, then there is leadership training after." They are pretty much in training "all the time." This is a true statement. Brevard County offers leadership and self improvement programs all the time, for all their employees. Brevard has 10 to 15 employees apply for the principal program each year; people who wish to improve their skills and are considering the position of principal in the future. They are transitioning to a Formal Coaching and

Mentoring Program because "research bears out and has shown enhanced mentoring will be required." As always, Hall looks to the future, as does Dr. DiPatri.

Why make a big fuss over a succession plan? Hall explains — "Without a succession plan, school districts could be: one promotion, one retirement, one demotion, one health-related incident, one winning lottery ticket away from disaster. Succession planning allows the momentum and inertia of existing leadership to continue long after the current leader is gone."

I think it is safe to say that Brevard County Schools' leaders know and understand the value of great principals.

Another program for Brevard's new principals is in its third year. The program is run by Bob Donaldson, a 44 year veteran principal who retired but came back to Brevard under contract to help new leaders succeed.

"Bob works with, and mentors, the first-year principals for three years. He mentors, coaches, guides, and gives advice." Hall said that what Bob and his first-year principals talk about is totally private which keeps all first-years safe in their positions and at the same time "this part of the program is imperative because it helps the administration learn what the first-year principals need to better themselves in their leadership. Bob cannot talk about any individual with anyone unless it is something illegal or immoral." This creates a trusting relationship between mentor and first-year principals.

Hall said that trust in the mentoring program is important and gave an example of how this works: Let us say I am a first-year principal. I know I can trust Bob Donaldson so I explain how I am frustrated with the budgeting for my school. I cannot seem to get priorities correct with budgeting and resources for my teachers. Bob sees I need help in that particular area of my position, so he makes a phone call to Hall and says, "Bill, we need a budgeting program." Hall then sets up classes for budgeting. Once the program is ready, Bob comes to me. "Tena," Bob says, "there's a budgeting program offered. Why don't you sign up for it?"

Obviously, this works for various reasons, and the out-come is success.

I learned from Hall that you can look on the internet for succession planning and management and you will find various sites, all having to do with corporate management and business. If you look for succession planning and management in public education, you will find nothing. In Hall's power-point he explains that "succession planning should not and must not stand alone. It must be paired with succession management which creates a more dynamic environment."

In order for you to do the best job possible, you need a mentor. There are those who are natural leaders, but even if you are one of those natural leaders, a mentor is a good confidante, a good friend, and the one person that will most likely save your sanity on those crazy and demanding days.

Future Outlook

When Hall was asked if the role of school principal has drastically changed over the years his immediate response was, "Oh God, has it ever." What does he see in the future?

"Better relationships with universities on what our principals need. We have to have communication, just as principals have to know how to communicate, how to budget, and they need more experience in many areas."

Brevard is working with one of the Florida universities on sending data from the schools regarding what principals are missing and in what areas they are succeeding. "Leadership has changed," said Hall, and he is right. "They are going to have to learn how to read data, learn how to use it, and be capable of data decision making. Principals need to partner with someone and get exposed to the data. Principals are now responsible for how well they do in creating capacity under their leadership. They have to develop leadership beneath them, and the people who are trained will be able to step in when it is time or it is needed."

It is obvious that principals are no longer managers. "They are now expected to be instructional leaders' first, managers second," explains Hall. It is important for principals to stay on top of new technology and curriculums; there are more changes to come. With the many assorted hats you now wear, you will learn to make room in your closet for more. With most states having new leadership and mentoring programs, all the information we've given you to ingest, with all the advice you have been given and the advice you will continue to get, there is a good chance you are well on your way to being a good leader.

There is hope that now the states and districts are realizing the importance of excellent principals. They are finally seeing the tremendous pressure principals are under, the demands they must meet, the from every angle the position brings, and the need for assistants which is now greater than ever before.

While it is important that you, as a principal, stay focused on what is best for the students and school community. It is just as important that you remember to take care of yourself. Do not be afraid to ask for help and delegate responsibilities. This has become necessary for all principals.

There have been numerous changes in the role of principal over the past ten years, but the vision of what is to come is that responsibilities will be even greater. The National Association of Elementary School Principals (NAESP) has a "Vision 2021 Project." In this vision they "study the future of principalship and the trends and issues of what they think is to come. Digital learning technologies will change the way teachers teach and students learn," reports NAESP from a survey of principals. It is said that principals are wondering if technology will weed out brick and mortar schools. Other studies say the institutions still have multiple values that people desire.

Another requirement of principals today is that they "globalize curriculums" to prepare students for global citizenry. This concept gave principals something more to think about; the need to educate students on multiculturalism. Another major concern is funding and budgets. With the nation having to address so many financial problems, the future of the schools and students is a major concern. Uneven per pupil funding across the country is already a problem. And with jobs leaving the country the problem looks like it will continue to worsen.

Another possibility for schools and principals future outlook is School-Based Management. School-Based Management decentralizes control from the central district office to individual schools. More and more school districts are going with School-Based Management, which puts more time-consuming burdens, and decisions, on the principals.

One thing to keep in mind while thinking of the future outlook for principals; even though there are going to be more responsibilities, it is now not only acceptable, but suggested, that principals share the burden of those responsibilities. Another optimistic point to bear in mind is that legislatures, states, and district offices are finally admitting that due to the amount of responsibilities principals need assistants, and sometimes more than one.

8
YOUNG IN HEART, AGED IN WISDOM

It is because of the number of decisions a principal must make each day, and the tremendous amount of responsibility that comes with the job, that we asked a number of principals if they would be kind enough to give some advice on the many different aspects of the job. Now we are going to share what they had to say, and we will begin with how best to manage your first-year as principal and avoid the mistakes that are most common.

Decisions or Common Mistakes

When asked what are the most common mistakes made by first-year principals, the answers overwhelmingly refered to making decisions and managing time. It is readily visible to anyone who would wish to shadow the principal during their normal workday that free time is nonexistent and making decisions is constant. Veteran Principal, Nancy Graham of Naples High School, Naples, Florida, said, "New principals tend to think they must have all the answers all of the time. The best advice given to me at the start of my administrative career was that very few decisions need to be made immediately. I've lived by that, and it has served me well."

Snap decisions are like snap judgments in that they are usually wrong. If you are dealing with two students who were in an altercation it may take some time to figure it out. Finding what is true and what is simply someone's perspective is important when dealing with such an incident. It is no different when you are dealing with a parent who makes a complaint about a teacher, or a staff member complaining about a new rule. Take your time in making a decision, give yourself the extra minutes, hours, or even days, to think the situation over and look at it from every angle.

Principal Robert Spano of Mike Davis Elementary in Naples, Florida, advises first-years to beware of "trying to do too much yourself. Be a good listener to your staff. Don't make decisions in isolation. Form committees or small groups of staff to discussion prior to making decisions."

Sharing the burden of all those decisions will make your position so much easier and enjoyable. Another bonus to the sharing of choices is building relationships with your staff. By sharing decisions you are bringing your staff on board your ship of dreams, welcoming them to share your vision and goals. All of these factors are important to you as a principal and as a person.

James Gasparino, Principal of Pelican Marsh Elementary in Naples, Florida, said, "Perhaps the most common mistakes made by first-year principals involve decision making. Principals have to make decisions all the time. Some are managerial in nature: some of far reaching consequences. First-year principals need to recognize that not all decisions need to be made immediately. It is necessary to be able to differentiate what needs to be settled right away, and what situations require reflection and input from others. First-year principals may want to do everything right away, and by themselves. It is difficult, if not impossible, to get buy-in from others if they didn't have a voice in the decision making process."

Gasparino has been a principal for 21 years and knows that making your staff part of your team is how you give them access to "have a voice in the decision making process." It is also how you get them to be part of the vision and goals you have set.

Principal Fielding had much to say about first-year principals taking on too much in the way of making decisions. As a veteran principal he has seen the changes that have taken place in the position of principal, and is aware of the many decisions a principal must make. "Beginning principals almost always fall into the trap of feeling like they need to be everything to everybody. It is important to understand that you cannot do that, either physically, academically, or emotionally. If you're too tired to move you are no good to anybody else. You do not really have to know and do everything yourself. That said, you do need to know those things that do require your attention and those that you can let others handle. Granted, this is a lot easier to say once you have some experience, but the advice is still to try to get to that point as soon as you can."

Building a team is not expected of you immediately. If you have never been inside the school where you are now the leader, or you have never worked with any of the staff who are now under your wing, it is impossible for a first-year to go into a school and instantly know who they can trust. Taking Fielding's advice in trying to get to that point as soon as possible is in your best interest, and will make your school run much smoother, much sooner.

Fielding also suggests, "It is important to pick your battles. I always use the measuring stick of 'is it good for kids' to help me decide what to fight about and what to let go. There will always be one more silly thing that somebody thinks is important but, does it really help kids in a significant way? I feel it is far more important to concentrate on people and building relationships than what program is best for this or that. Kids and parents, and even most teachers, pretty much do not really care what reading or math program you are using, but they all care very much about your relationship with them."

"It is better to take your time before reacting to a situation," advises Principal Redd. "It will give you a different perspective if you take the time to get all the facts before making a hasty decision."

Jory Westbury of Tommie Barfield Elementary has been principal for seven years. Tommie Barfield is located on Marco Island, Florida, and Westbury oversees 700 students. Principal Westbury advises first-year principals to first avoid "thinking you should have all the answers," and secondly, avoid "thinking you should be able to make all decisions quickly." She also advises that you should never think you know more than your staff or that you're better than anyone else.

Managing time is of the essence for a first-year principal. This is important so that you do not burn out before you even get started. Five-year veteran, Pamela C. Mitchell, is principal at Central Middle School in West Melbourne, Florida, and she says it is a common mistake to forget "that there are 24 hours in a day. You will never catch up! Set a time to end your day, go home and relax. If you take your work home, make it something that you need to do for tomorrow — you will feel like you accomplished something." Mitchell also advises that first-year principals not make the mistake in thinking that "change is easy. Open your eyes more than your mouth," she said.

According to Principal Belanger, another common mistake for first-years is "feeling like you can do everything yourself. You can avoid this by finding out who you can delegate to, but make sure it is someone who can still keep you informed and updated on what you need to know. Also, find other principals who you can call on to help you find answers to those unknown questions you meet up with."

Making quick changes as a first-year principal is another common mistake made by first-years that most of our principals mentioned. Veteran principal for 25 years, Chet Sanders of The Professional Academies at Loften in Gainesville, Florida, said, "Getting started immediately with making changes before taking time to really study the school community" is one common mistake he has seen.

Principal Pichard advises that all first-years will make a mistake by "forgetting how it is to walk in a teacher's shoes. Principals, not only first-years, but as we mature need to remember how it is in the classroom. It is one of the toughest jobs around." Teachers must deal with "many demands from administrators, parents, and the students themselves."

Roy Miller is a principal in Knoxville, Tennessee, and most of his students are project kids. Poor, from broken homes, and in need of assistance, Miller knows what it is like to have to budget, scrounge for resources, work with diversity, and make daily decisions. He has been principal of Moorland Heights Elementary for five years and feels that "the number one mistake is to go into a school and not learn both the culture and the 'hidden' culture of the building. It is important to just sit back, listen and learn. I think it is also good to earn and give respect."

Principal Michael Miller of Saturn Elementary in Cocoa, Florida, said, "Many first-years want to make too many changes too quickly. Some also feel they have to do everything by themselves. The biggest one (mistake) is to come on too strong and feel they have to show who is boss. If you have to ever remind them who the boss is, you have a problem."

The advice you just read was given by principals who have held the position of school leader for five to 25 years. These are veterans who have been there, done that, and are well aware of what you are walking into.

We also questioned some first-year principals who are presently going through what you are about to, or are just now facing. These principals have tenacity, integrity, and are learning how to cope in a short span of time. When asked how they were managing to handle all the responsibilities as a first-year principal they were united in that it was more than they were expecting, but so far, bearable. Katherine Munn, principal of Littlewood Elementary in Gainesville, Florida, advises first-years to "just work really hard and very long hours. My 14-year-old daughter tells me she wants me to get a job at McDonald's so I can be home more." Munn also said, "Work hard and delegate the things that you can so you can work on the important things."

Tret Witherspoon is a first-year principal at a small, rural, public school in Crawfordville, Georgia. At Taliaferro County Charter School where Witherspoon is now leader, he has already learned much about being a principal. His best advice of what is important for first-years? "Great time management and delegating responsibilities to others on the leadership team. It is impossible for one person to complete all the required assignments. In addition, it provides an opportunity for others to utilize their leadership abilities. I also synchronize my smart phone with my calendar on Outlook to keep up with appointments and other important assignments. Prioritize responsibilities. Search out teachers who have an interest in leadership and put them to work."

Tammy Brown is a first-year principal in Naples, Florida. There are 953 students in the Sabal Palm Elementary where she is presently getting her feet wet with leadership. When discussing the burdensome responsibilities on principals Brown said to handle them, "one at a time. I try to do the paperwork and office task early in the morning or after dismissal so that I can be in classrooms, halls and cafeteria interacting with teachers and students as much as possible. There is often something that comes up that must be dealt with immediately but most often things can be prioritized." Brown advises you, "Try not to do everything in your inbox every day. It is okay to leave something for the next day."

Another principal I would like to introduce is ten-year veteran, Oliver. I personally spoke with Principal Phipps and was most impressed with his sincerity. He loves his job at Estates Elementary in Naples, Florida, his staff, and his 668 students. When I asked him what he felt was the most common mistake made by first-year principals his immediate response was, "change." Phipps thinks it is important that new principals, "sit back and watch. If the teachers loved the previous principal, why can it not work for you?"

Phipps was a first-year principal at Golden Gate Elementary. He took over at a place where "the previous principal had been there for ten years." I remember hearing the secretary say, "I don't know if I can work for him. He's a baby." I just watched and took notes, talked with the teachers and waited until we were halfway through the year before I even talked about change." Phipps was smart and took his time, suggesting a different way of doing something or asking for opinions on a new idea. "It was the second year before I made any changes," he said.

As discovered by speaking with veteran principals, in your line of work decisions must be made every day. This does not mean you must make all the decisions by yourself, and it does not mean you cannot hand over some of the responsibilities which require decisions. You will get to know your teachers and you will find where their skills and talents lay hidden or unused. These are the people you want to have on your team, helping you to attain the dreams, visions and goals you set for the students of your school.

When looking at advising principals and their words of wisdom it must be said that the two factors found in common among these leaders was the heart and respect they carry for their students and staff. The more I conversed with them, the easier it became to ascertain that their heart, their sincerity, and their integrity was what makes them phenomenal leaders in education. While there are some school communities who have the misfortune of acquiring principals who are not good leaders, it is apparent the school communities that have the principals I have interviewed are fortunate indeed. It has given me hope for our students today and the students of tomorrow, and restored my faith in humanity.

Excellent Leaders and Their Advice

The following opinions and advice are from first-year principals, all of whom were hired to start their position for the school year of 2007-2008. These principals were previously introduced, but their information, along with more facts about their schools, is listed again. Heed their advice, which is based on what they have learned during their first year as a leader of an educational establishment. It seems important to point out that their answers will vary according to what is available to them in their district, the demographics of the community in which they work, and the budgeting allowances available. There are other factors that determine their decisions, and as a principal, or soon-to-be principal, you will understand this first-hand.

- Tammy Brown, first-year principal at Sabal Palm Elementary. Brown started her position as principal in March 2007, and has responsibility for 953 students in this suburban, public school in Collier County, Florida.

- Katherine Munn, first-year principal at Littlewood Elementary. Munn has responsibility for 433 students in this public, urban school in Gainesville, Florida.

- Tret Witherspoon, first-year principal at Taliaferro County Charter School. Witherspoon has responsibility for 238 students in this small, rural, public establishment located in Crawfordville, Georgia.

Question: *As a first-year principal how did you assess the institution and choose curriculums?*

> **Brown:** "Our district has a data warehouse which has updated demographics, test results, and School Improvement plans available to view. Those were used as a starting point. Teachers assess students frequently, and report their progress through class data sheets. We meet to discuss the information on those sheets, to determine if the district curriculums and materials are being successful, or if intervention strategies are needed. Our district has committees to select curriculum materials from a state approved list. We use research based intervention materials as well."

> **Munn:** "The curriculums in our district are used by all the schools. Each school has a representative on the committee. For example, this year we are in process of choosing a reading series. Every school had the opportunity to have a member on the committee. Each school representative brought back the top three choices to their schools and the faculty voted on their top choice. We also used our Title ! funds to host an after-school tutoring program for our lowest quartile of students. That curriculum is chosen by the teachers."

> **Witherspoon:** "I accessed the institution by evaluating past year's data, including attendance. I also interviewed present teachers to find their opinion of school climate, curriculum, discipline, scheduling, parent involvement, etc. Many of the curriculum and instructional ideas came from ideas from my previous school where I served as assistant principal. I also received input from our Regional Educational Service Agency (RESA), and from the Georgia State Leadership Facilitator."

Question: *How do you determine the best resources for your teachers?*

Brown: "Many times it comes from the teachers themselves. If they see materials or workshops of interest and they are in alignment with our school and district goals, we look for funds from our Parent Teacher Organization, Grants, or School Improvement funds to support teachers."

Munn: "Curriculum Council (Team Leaders) and I chose which the best is. Teachers know that when they come to me with a special order that it has to be research-based."

Witherspoon: "Best resources are always determined by researched proven resources and by talking with other school administrators that have used the resources."

Question: *What is your strategy for implementing new curriculums and what advice would you give other first-year principals for implementing new curriculums in their school?*

Brown: "First, teachers are asked to look at the materials and maps before implementing. Teachers are encouraged to help write curriculum maps for the district as well as serve on district curriculum teams and provide input. Our school has curriculum committees to support each other in implementation as well. Advice to others in implementing new curriculums: Involve teachers in decision making and exploration as much as possible. Provide training in curriculum mapping as needed."

Munn: "When the district chooses a new curriculum, they offer extensive in-services for that new curriculum. Advice to others in implementing new curriculums: Let the teachers have input, so they are stakeholders, and be sure that there is plenty of opportunity for staff development of the new curriculums."

Witherspoon: "I would recommend doing an environmental scan of your present school's curriculum to see what works and what doesn't work. There may not be a need for a complete overhaul. Next I would talk with other school principals and curriculum directors to see what works for them and why. Networking is always key."

Question: *In your personal opinion, how can a first-year principal lead and support his or her faculty best?*

Brown: "Listening and observing are two very important things to do first. Each school has a unique culture and way of doing things. It is important to respect the current culture. Any changes that need to be made can be made by empowering staff and working with people's strengths to make an organization stronger."

Munn: "I think that it is important for a first year principal to 'fit into the school,' not have the school fit into your beliefs. The faculty and staff need to know that you are supportive of them and they can trust you."

Witherspoon: "Principals win support best by listening to their teachers. Principals must first win their support by listening to opinions and ideas. Teachers must have a stake in decision making. When teachers have a stake in the decision making, it encourages 'buy in.' "

Question: *Do you feel mutual respect is important in achieving your goals in successfully managing an educational institution?*

Brown: "Extremely important because with mutual respect comes trust. In our world we need to rely on one another and be able to be innovating and try new things. Without trust, that can be quite difficult. I need my staff to trust that I will make the best decisions possible and that I respect their opinions as professionals. I cannot be all places at all times and I need to trust and respect teachers, and know that they are following through on our school goals and doing what is best for children."

Munn: "I feel that it is a huge role in it but your staff also needs to know that ultimately the responsibility falls on you."

Witherspoon: "I feel as though mutual respect is vital in achieving goals in successfully managing an educational institution. Your staff will not respect you if you do not respect them. All deserve to be respected. The philosophy goes with any leadership role."

Question: *Where do you obtain feedback on your performance as a principal?*

Brown: "Informally through conversations with teachers, students and staff members. I have an open door and enjoy brainstorming sessions. Formally our teacher union can do a performance review and the superintendent does an evaluation as well."

Munn: "The staff already completed a School Advisory Council (SAC) survey and I will put out a personal survey at the end of the school year."

Witherspoon: "Feedback is obtained through online generated surveys. The surveys must be made confidential."

Question: *Do you have concerns on state laws and litigations, and if yes, please explain.*

Brown: "The laws that require the most attention usually involve issues regarding special needs situations. I do not personally have concerns but I do work diligently to stay in compliance with the technical aspects of individual educational plans. I also try to read current law cases because you never know what might apply to you on any given day. There are people in our district office to guide me through any 'sticky' situations."

Munn: "Yes, on class size reduction. The state of Florida voted to only have a certain number of students in each class and that causes a big problem when you have new students register and you have to fit them in classes that you have no room for growth in."

Witherspoon: "Yes. When I have a concern about whether or not I am in compliance with state and federal law, I first turn to the Internet for answers. Our district subscribes to E-Law, which is an online based legal consultant. If I'm still in doubt about a concern, I turn to the Superintendent for suggestions. I try not to bother my superintendent unless necessary."

Question: *With respect for each situation being different, are there one or two crucial factors in dealing with conflict?*

Brown: "In any kind of conflict I feel it is important to listen first. Usually the concern is the last to come out when someone is upset. Identifying the issue and then addressing the issue in a calm and objective way usually works best."

Munn: "I try to be fair and equable."

Witherspoon: "One crucial factor is to not take sides. Find out the root of the problem and offer solutions. Never blame anyone for the conflict, even if it is obvious. Employees appreciate that."

Question: *How do you feel your success as a leader will be judged and how do you measure your own success?*

Brown: "With state testing such a priority it would seem to reason that my success is based on student achievement. It could also be judged on teacher retention vs. turn over. My success may also be judged on both the climate and condition of the school."

How do you measure your own success? "I judge success by seeing students and staff grow. I want everyone to achieve more and learn more than the day before. I want them to do this because it is fun not out of obligation."

Munn: "I think mostly by word of mouth. How happy the staff and parents. Also (unfortunately) by the school grade." How do you measure your own success? "This year it will be by the staff and parent surveys and unfortunately the school grade."

Witherspoon: "My success will be judged based on the improvement students show on standardized tests (hands down)." How do you measure your own success? "I measure my own success by improvement in test scores, professional growth of teachers', school culture and climate, satisfied parents, and happy students."

Question: *Do you have any suggestions as to how the states could better protect principals and teachers?*

Brown: "No suggestions."

Munn: "Allocate more money to education."

Witherspoon: "Continual staff development support. School administrators and teachers cannot have enough. Also by measuring other factors that will measure success other than domains from NCLB."

Question: *Could you share any suggestions as to how the states could better handle the firing process of bad teachers?*

Brown: "It is very difficult to remove a tenured teacher who is ineffective. This comes from the bargaining agreements and unions. We do have a process in place but it takes a lot of time and effort. It seems there could be an easier way to remove someone."

Munn: "Probably make it a little easier. It really takes so much to get rid of low performing teachers. In the schools that I have worked in I haven't seen that many but there are a few."

Witherspoon: "This process is handled fairly well in the State of Georgia. Administrators must allow for teachers to improve delivery of instruction through a professional development plan (PDP). If, after a period of time, the teacher does not improve, the principal then gathers documentation for dismissal. This is the procedure for tenured teachers. The overall goal should be not to renew inadequate teachers whom do not have tenure."

Question: *As a first-year principal what do you most hope to achieve?*

Brown: "When I began my role as principal, the staff here wanted to feel more connected to one another. I worked hard to set the tone that we would be a team all working together for the success of all students. We have a good feeling here that we are all part of a team, but mostly as grade level or department teams. I am still working on us being one big team. That was challenging with 30 new teachers to the school this year. Next year we will continue. I will feel successful when we meet that goal and I hear all staff members talk about the students, not as mine or yours, but as ours."

Munn: "At this point to maintain an A as the school grade. I feel that I already have most of the faculty and staff on board with me. That is important."

Witherspoon: "I hope to achieve APY status for my school. This has never happened before."

Question: *Do you have a mentor? Please share something about him or her.*

Brown: "Yes, both formally and informally. One is a director in the district office and one is a principal. They both have several years of principal experience." What is the best advice he or she has given you? "When faced with a difficult, but obvious decision, and I wanted to be sure I was doing the right thing, my mentor told me the best way to handle the situation was head on. If I felt strongly about my decision it wasn't going to help to wait and communicate my decision but to just do it."

Munn: "Yes, Alachua County assigns you one as a first year principal. Ms. Donna Jones has been wonderful. She sits down and explains things to me and has helped me out many times this year." What is the best advice he or she has given you? "Probably about giving teachers Professional Service Contact. She said that I needed to be sure that I would want them to teach for me for the next 30 years before I offer them it."

Witherspoon: "I do not have a mentor, but could desperately use one. My school is the only school in the district."

Question: *What do you feel is your biggest challenge as a principal?*

Brown: "I would love to have more time to get to know the families on a more personal level."

Munn: "Making EVRYONE happy. It is an impossible task. I know that it cannot be done but I want everyone know that I do listen to their concerns and do the best that I can to solve problems."

Witherspoon: "Finding the time to complete all the day to day operations of being a principal."

Question: *What challenges do you see for new principals in the future?*

Brown: "Keeping up with technology. It is amazing what we have in classrooms but also what students use daily such as I-pods and cell phones."

Munn: "Just the amount of responsibility being put on the educational system. There are new mandates all the time but very few things are being taken away. It is hard to continue to do everything that is asked."

Witherspoon: "As accountability requirements for NCLB continue to increase, so will the challenges of meeting AYP. Just like athletic coaches, school principals will be put under pressure to turn around and maintain AYP status."

Question: *Please share your reason for becoming a principal.*

Brown: "As a teacher I didn't set out to be a principal but often found myself in leadership roles. I had a principal who saw that in me and encouraged me. I was intrigued by the idea of being able to reach more students by reaching teachers. I love people!"

Munn: "Ever since my first day of teaching, I knew that I wanted to be a principal. I don't know why-it was just my dream."

Witherspoon: "By serving as a principal, I am able to have a greater impact on the learning by involving all stakeholders and generating a nurturing school culture and climate."

Question: *In achieving success for your educational institution how important are your teachers?*

Brown: "They are the most important and influential part of student achievement."

Munn: "The teachers are the heart of the system."

Witherspoon: "Teachers are priority! They are the driving force for your school. Great teachers = great students."

Question: *How well do you feel college prepared you for your first year as principal? What are two or three facts you would have liked to have learned in college before becoming a principal?*

Brown: "Just like preparing you to be a teacher, the best learning comes on the job. College helped with the law and finance and managerial tasks. Since no day is ever the same as the one before, you never know exactly what to prepare for each morning."

Munn: "My Educational Leadership Degree taught me many things (Financial, Curriculum, Law) but not how to deal with difficult parents."

Witherspoon: I would have liked to have learned more on "how to involve community stakeholders in the decision making process; evaluating teachers and staff; managing extracurricular activities such as athletic events; creating a disaster prevention management plan."

Question: *It has been noted that the schools are constantly being watched by groups and politicians for their own beneficial reasons. A few of these people are legislators and the media. Please give your advice, or an analogy, on this constant surveillance for personal gain.*

Brown: "News media loves a good story. I can attest to that. One day, early on in my new role, we had a problem with the water and the toilets didn't flush. We had trucks of water being shipped in, bottled water for drinking and luckily it was an early release day. Instead of the news media focusing on what the cause was or how the community may have rallied to our aide, they chose to take pictures of the dirty toilets."

Munn: "I really don't have much of an opinion on this. It is a shame that everyone doesn't have the view of the children should come first."

Witherspoon: "Anyone that's on the outside looking in is eager to exert his or her two cents in. All politicians should spend a couple of weeks in a school to get an inside perspective of the day to day on goings of a school."

Question: *How would you define your role as principal?*

Brown: "My role is first and foremost that of an instructional leader, and guiding staff through the process of analyzing data and creating engaging lessons for students. Of course there are numerous roles that must be fulfilled as well: communication with stakeholders (staff, community, parents, and students) to keep us working as a team, manager of resources and personnel, maintenance of facility and working closely with custodial and trades people to have quality facilities."

Munn: "I feel that I am the curriculum leader of the school. I am a facilitator and mediator between parents, community, faculty and staff."

Witherspoon: "I would describe myself as the instructional leader of my school. I am also in charge of maintenance, discipline, school improvement, etc."

Experiences of Exceptional Leaders

Now to turn to some veteran principals who are most impressive in their role as educational leaders. These principals have very little free time, but gave openly of that priceless time to help you, as a first-year, so that you may have a better idea of what to expect. You have already been introduced to some of these leaders, but we will give their information again, starting with youngest in years as principal, and working to those who have been doing this job for a very long time. These leaders, one and all, have good advice and definitive suggestions for making your life as a principal, and your endless demands, a little easier.

- Roy Miller is a five-year veteran principal at Mooreland Heights Elementary. Miller has responsibility for 330 students in this small, urban school located in Knoxville, Tennessee.

- Barbara A. Belanger is a five-year veteran principal at Harbor City Elementary. Belanger is responsible for 470 students in this small, suburban school located in Melbourne, Florida.

- Pamela C. Mitchell, a five-year veteran principal at Central Middle School in West Melbourne, Florida, oversees 1,000 students. These students fall under Mitchell's care in this large, urban school.

- Jory Westbury is a seven-year veteran principal at Tommie Barfield Elementary. At this public school of 700 students on Marco Island, Florida, Westbury stands watch.

- Michael D. Miller is a nine-year veteran principal. Miller has responsibility for 750 students at Saturn Elementary, a rural, public school in Cocoa, Florida.

- Oliver Phipps, a ten-year veteran principal takes care of his students at his public, educational establishment of 668 students. Phipps stands watch over his learners and staff at Estates Elementary, which is located in Naples, Florida.

- Dr. Nancy J. Graham is a veteran leader of 13 years. She is the principal at Naples High School in Naples, Florida.

- An exceptional principal, Barry Pichard, is a 15-year veteran. Pichard is responsible for 750 students at the Sunrise Elementary, a public school located in Palm Bay, Florida.

- Veteran principal of 16 years, Robert Spano, is steadfast in his watch over Mike Davis Elementary students. Mike Davis is a suburban, public school of 550 students, and is located in Naples, Florida.

- Dr. Leonard Weiss is a 20-year veteran principal. He leads The A. Quinn Jones Center which provides a therapetic environment for 120 enotionally disturbed students. Located in Gainesville, Florida, Dr. Weiss has ovenseen this special school since 1994.

- The Pelican Marsh Elementary School houses 780 students who are led by the 21-year veteran principal, Dr. James A. Gasparino. Located in Naples, Florida, Pelican Marsh Elementary is a public, suburban school.

- The excellent leader, John Fielding, is a 21-year veteran principal in Gainesville, Florida. Fielding oversees approximately 630 students in the suburban, public school of Idylwild Elementary. Fielding points out that Idylwild's number of students "changes every day," and this keeps him on constant watch.

- Chet Sanders, a 25-year veteran leader stands sentinel over 225 students at The Professional Academies at Loften, a small, suburban, public school located in Gainesville, Florida.

- In Bellevue, Ohio, John Redd is a great leader and is responsible for the 312 students at the Bellevue Junior High School.

Question: *What do you feel is the biggest challenge facing today's principals?*

Phipps: "Maintaining morale. There's always something, like a lack of funding, paperwork to keep organized, dealing with so many tests, laws, changes… It's hard to keep upbeat and stay focused. Another problem is maintaining the state assessment grade."

Roy Miller: "The change in expectation from society as a whole. The school has now become a 'service center' that is expected to meet more than the academic needs of the children. We are bombarded with having to 'pick up where the parents leave off. This sometimes causes us to go into the lives of children far beyond the educational realm. I know teachers, at times, feel that they are more of a social worker than an educator."

Belanger: "Trying to maintain the position of instructional leader while often being out of the loop on curriculum and instructional materials. Much of this information is shared with Assistant Principals at their district meetings. As a principal, you have to really be proactive in keeping up with state adopted materials and district assessments."

Mitchell: "The biggest challenge is maintaining the morale of your best teachers."

Michael Miller: "Accountability pressures from the high stakes testing and just being able to keep up with everything you are in charge of. Just looking at the amount of paper that crosses my desk on a daily basis is overwhelming. Being able to keep track of where it came from, where you put it, and when it is due can be overwhelming. I have constantly looked to the one system that can organize me the best. I have come to the realization that I am probably the most organized of my friends."

Graham: "The dynamic tension between the role of leader and manager is the greatest challenge. There is a need for visionary leadership in today's public schools, and the crisis management that is unavoidable can really get in the way unless a principal chooses his administrator team wisely; a combination of skills is needed to be able to develop and carry through with the vision while still maintaining/managing the day to day operation of the school house."

Pichard: "Parents and 'community' expectations. Parents and the "community" expect the schools to solve everything. Parents often expect the school to change their students because of their bad parenting skills. Parents have changed dramatically in the last five years. Before I would have the students who were rude and disrespectful to teachers, and school staff. Now the students are taking their cue from their best teachers... the parents, because they see them being rude and disrespectful to school staff when they are at conferences, meetings, etc. The community also blames all the social woes and problems on the schools because we are a good target. We do not defend our school enough when the public prints articles, etc... because the majority of our students come to school, do their work each day, have no problems, earn scholarships, etc... but the community sometimes only sees the students who make the newspaper or TV news."

Spano: "NCLB and state assessments."

Weiss: "The biggest challenge facing principals today is recruiting qualified teachers to work with our ever changing student population. I work in a K-12 Center school for students with emotional behavioral disabilities. There is an increase in students with severe problems who need teachers to meet their special needs."

Gasparino: "The biggest challenge for first year principals is securing and maintaining the confidence and trust form the public, faculty, and school district."

Fielding: "I think the biggest challenge is finding the very best teachers that you can to meet the needs of your students. I will sometimes interview 30 teachers before finding just the right one that will fit the needs of a particular group of students. There were probably many of that group that will be good teachers, but for some reason I felt they weren't a 'good fit.' I tell teachers that a fair amount of my job is trying to keep the nonsense away from them. By nonsense, I mean things like politics, silly rules handed down from on high, all the extraneous things that the outside folks think would be a wonderful idea for schools, e.g. every service club, environmental group, charitable organization, etc. thinks a poster contest is a wonderful and original idea. In Florida the Department of Education is constantly changing and every change brings a fresh set of rules. Interestingly enough, almost none of them have any real impact on schools if the principal is willing to not get stressed by whatever they are saying. By the way, that's really hard if not impossible to do unless you have a supportive Board and superintendent above you."

Sanders: "Providing the leadership to develop in your teachers the desire to work collaboratively with each other to continually improve one another's practice."

Redd: "Getting student to be motivated. This often times is a result up their upbringing."

Question: *How well does college prepare you for your job as principal?*

Phipps: "Not well. Being a good principal is mostly on-the-job training. For instance, having a parent cursing you out wasn't in Principal Training 101. Training for the curriculum is there, the paperwork, but the nuts and bolts, you do not get that until you are in this seat."

Roy Miller: "I think as well as can be expected. However, there is nothing better than experience and 'hands on' experience.' "

Belanger: "Not very well, I am afraid, especially in the areas of facilities and human resources."

Mitchell: "There is no college course nor classroom teaching experience that prepares you for the job as principal. Today's principal must be everything to all people, including parents, community business persons and leaders, attorneys, media, etc. Oh yes — did I say teachers and students?"

Michael Miller: "Not much. I believe each district has a training program that better prepares you for being a Principal than college."

Graham: "I am unsure anything can truly prepare one for this job except for 'time in the chair.' I took only one course in personnel, and that was at the doctoral level. Ironically, a large bulk of a principal's time is spent dealing with personnel issues. It's a myth that children create the most challenging times for a principal."

Pichard: "I felt that my college, Frostburg State, did prepare me for the role of being a principal. However, in Brevard County Florida when you are an assistant principal you apply to enter a Preparing New Principal's Program. This was a two year program with meetings including your building principal, mentor principal from another school and the Area Superintendent. This program provided a lot of experiences before applying to become a school principal. This program also helps when Area Superintendents are selecting a new principal for a building in that they may already know what experiences of an individual."

Spano: "There is no experience better than hands on. Book experience is not any where near the same as actual school experience."

Weiss: "College gives you a theoretical basis for your practice. However, most of what you learn is through experience, in other words on the job training."

Gasparino: "University work, particularly at the advanced degree level, does help prepare as for the principalship in providing the necessary academic and theoretical knowledge needed. However, the necessary experiential knowledge can only be gained through on the job training, such as serving as an assistant principal under a good mentor."

Fielding: "I'm sure that depends on the college you attend. In my experience there was very little in my 'formal training in principal school' that has ever been useful. Except, I guess, learning to jump through hoops is occasionally helpful. Pretty much everything I know and use on a daily basis has been learned through on the job training or in talking with other principals. Of course my BA and M.Ed. are in special education, and I had little formal training in educational leadership until the doctorate program. Other colleges may provide excellent experience."

Sanders: "College coursework provides a good foundation in many areas that the principal deals with. However, much of the knowledge that principals need must be learned over time with experience."

Redd: "College gives you some basic knowledge, but much of what you need to know, you find out on the job and from your teaching experience."

Question: *Name two or three things you would have preferred to have known before starting the job as principal.*

Phipps: "I think it would have been nice to have been given latitude to learn the job.

Roy Miller: "The expectations of the teachers, parents, and central office are three that come to mind."

Belanger: "1.) How to interview personnel more effectively in positions such as custodians and cafeteria staff. I think principals are pretty good at interviewing instructional personal as well as office staff, but cafeteria and custodial positions are usually ones we have never held.

"2.) How to work with the local media in a crisis situation. Our district has done a good job of preparing principals once you are hired, but this is a position that many of us have not yet experienced until the media shows up on campus."

Mitchell: "No matter what you plan and how you plan it, your schedule is at the mercy of things that you cannot control — do not think that you are incompetent because you do not get to the bottom of your list.

"Students care about you — but they are also afraid (most students) of the authority they see in the position. If you want to get the pulse on your school — gain their trust. Spend more time talking with your students than you do in your office.

"Principals need to remember that teachers need constant affirmation that they are valuable."

Michael Miller: "How lonely it can feel being in charge and just knowing the amount of work that is expected every day."

Graham: "My biggest initial 'aha' as an administrator was that if I say it then it matters or must be true to those who hear it. The opportunity to just participate in a conversation with staff members disappeared as soon as I got my title."

Pichard: "I was an Assistant Principal for six and one-half years so I did realize the extent of the job. However, I guess when you are the 'keeper of the keys' of the building you have a whole different perspective of what happens in your building especially on your first day away from the building attending a meeting. The other item is the 'You are the final word' which is different when you are the AP. You can refer a decision to the principal when you are a subordinate. When you are the 'keeper of the keys' then the 'Buck

Stops Here' applies to only one sole person…YOU! and sometimes it is lonely when you are feeling like you are 'floating on the island' making decisions that may not be popular with staff, parents or community members."

Spano: "Be sure you are able to handle people second guessing your decisions and be prepared to spend easily 50-60 hours a week on the job."

Weiss: "1.) A better understanding of budgeting practices. 2) A better understanding of personnel practices."

Gasparino: "I would have liked to have known how much attention I would receive and being the topic of conversation I would become. Also, I would have liked to have known that I didn't have to do everything myself. In fact, my authority was enhanced when I realized that I should share it. Always remember that essentially we are in a people business. Also, I wish I knew when somebody screwed up, it became my problem and screw-up!"

Fielding: "Well,………ummmm………….I'm sure there MUST be something, but I can't really think of anything. When I got the first call that I was going to be a principal, I was pretty sure they must be kidding (but that's another story) so I didn't really have time to think about such things, and it was a LONG time ago."

Sanders: "I would have benefited from having been exposed to some of the comprehensive reform efforts such as Sizer's work with the Coalition of Essential Schools. Having examples of best practices that are producing positive results with students, helps principals build a vision for the kind of school they would like to aim towards."

Redd: "How difficult it would be to make sound decisions, and then stick by them."

Question: *Could you please share some words of wisdom passed to you which helped you get through the trying days of being a first year principal?*

Phipps: "I had a very good principal when I was an assistant principal. He was a great mentor. He helped me to understand budgeting and formulas for the hiring process. He taught me what to look for in a teacher. 'Look for the heart,' he told me. My dad, also a principal, always talked to me and told me to 'treat people with respect even when critiquing their work, do it in a respectful way. Help them instead of belittling them.' "

Roy Miller: "My director told me that the decisions that I make would take as long as 20 minutes my first year. However, as I begin to build a 'data base' of answers to questions, within a few years, those same questions will be answered in as little as three seconds."

Belanger: "Remember that you usually have made a situation a lot worse in your head then it actually is."

Mitchell: "The day will not last forever. Focus on the kids."

Michael Miller: "Call before you act. It is always easier to get advice than to clean up a mess."

Graham: "There are very few decisions that have to be made immediately. Stop what you are doing when someone walks in your office to see you. Their issue matters to them, and they need your undivided attention."

Pichard: "Make sure you take time for yourself… because you will need it. You can not run on all cylinders 24/7. (However, I am working on this aspect every day because some days you have to run 24 /7).”

Spano: “Respond to all communications, such as email and phone calls, on the day you receive them.”

Weiss: “1.) Never be bullied into making a decision before you have all the facts.

“2.) Delay immediately solving a problem, it may not be one tomorrow.

“3.) Treat everyone as an individual.

“4.) This too shall pass.”

Gasparino: “Some advice that I found valuable is to realize not to avoid problems. They won’t go away and probably become worse. Also, always realize that no matter what, parents love their children and try to do their best. They really do send you the best children they have and are not keeping the good ones at home.”

Fielding: “There are so many; most of what I know came from the lady who got me out of the classroom and into this little job. Come to think of it, she lives in Columbus, you really ought to talk to her! I guess some of the short bits include ‘Did somebody tell you life is fair?’ or ‘You can’t rationalize with an irrational person.’ ‘The madder the other person is, the calmer you have to be.’ ‘Never hire anybody dumber than you are.’ ‘The hardest thing you’ll ever do is count kids and balance teacher units.’ ”

Sanders: “If it is good for kids, the answer is yes.”

Redd: "Make a friend with another administrator and be able to share experiences. Make sure you open up to your spouse and not let things get bottled up once you go home."

Question: *What are your top personal priorities as a principal?*

Phipps: "Staffing, make sure it is complete with people who share your vision. Budget, make sure all monies are accounted for. Inventory, all is accounted for. Most importantly, make sure all the children are learning."

Roy Miller: "Two are 'hiring staff and individually placing children in the classroom.' "

Belanger: "1.) Safety of my students, 2.) Making sure we provide a learning environment that is non-threatening and supportive of student progress."

Mitchell: "I would like to leave a legacy of pride. I want students, parents, teachers, and community to see Central as an academic and aesthetic asset."

Michael Miller: "Safety and student achievement."

Graham: "Relationships between staff and students; between staff and staff; between staff and parents, etc. etc. Relationships matter. When they are in line, the other stuff all works out so much more smoothly."

Pichard: "Safety of students, all staff and parents. If students, staff and parents feel safe at our school then everything else should fall into place. Good learning, good teaching, satisfaction from the parents that their students are happy with our school and their progress in the academics."

Spano: "Support your staff. Create an environment that is safe and conducive to learning. Be able to listen and make good decisions based on what is best for your students."

Weiss: "Give teachers the support, materials and equipment and the confidence to do their job so that they can increase student achievement. To encourage parents to become involved in their child's education. To create a climate where teachers and administrators are on the same page and communicate with each staff member effectively. Don't loose sight of the ball, student achievement."

Gasparino: "My top priorities as a principal is to provide the best academic education I can for all my students, keep them physically and emotionally safe, and make them feel happy to come to my school."

Fielding: "Are the kids learning? Is the staff happy? Do they all love kids? Do they love their jobs? Do the parents and others describe us as a friendly school? Things like that. If the answers are a resounding YES, you know the answer to question 22. I could go into all the usual junk about test scores and student achievement, but if you can answer yes to questions like this, that stuff takes care of itself."

Sanders: "I want to make sure that none of my students leave without a diploma and the absolutely essential skills and knowledge he/she will need in either college or a career."

Redd: "My top priority is to make sure we have a safe and comfortable place to learn and grow."

Question: *How important are your teachers and how would you say it is best to use their abilities in your institution?*

Phipps: "Very important. Use all their gifts because one person cannot do it all. If you have a teacher who is good at power-point presentations, use them for it and give them recognition. My dad also told me, 'What is a leader? A servant.' Make sure your teachers have everything they need to keep afloat."

Roy Miller: "The school sinks or swims with the faculty that is in place in the building."

Belanger: "My teachers are the most important people on my campus. They are the ones that the students and parents see and communicate with first in any situation. When hiring you need to remember that the abilities of enthusiasm, commitment and team work are high on the priority list. Most other abilities can be taught."

Mitchell: "My teachers are very important. Even though the students are my priority, I could not fulfill my priorities without the cooperation from my teachers. I always look for the best in each teacher. I treat them as I would a student — not one is perfect, and if you look for the positive, you will find it. I place my teachers in a position and environment that best suits them so that they can be the best that they can be. I do not believe in forcing teachers to teach something that they do not want to teach, or be a part of a committee they do not want to be a part of. It took me four years to get that understanding across to my teachers, and I rarely run into resistance. If I do, I can usually reach a compromise (do it this year, semester, and next year I will do my best to give you what you want. So far I have been able to stick to my word — if I cannot deliver my word I have at least built a history of trust)."

Michael Miller: "Wow, they are the most important thing to student performance in the classroom. I told my teachers the first day on campus there would be millions of times I would rely on them to make the decision. Then there would be times I needed to make a decision and I would need their input before I made my decision. Lastly, there would be times I would have to make a decision and they would have to have the faith that I was doing what I thought was best."

Graham: "Teachers are the heart of the matter in a school. I am currently working with my staff to become a 'strengths-based' organization using the research from Gallup to better capitalize on the natural talents of folks instead of trying to force skills/abilities that may really just be unavailable!"

Pichard: "Teachers make it happen or not happen. They are in the trenches every day. They are the communicators with the parents on a daily basis. Students do better when they feel that their teacher respects them. In order to earn respect you have to give it first. So when teachers are professional and use good judgment it makes my job a lot easier."

Spano: "Teachers are the most important staff members in your building. They can work as a team and learn from one another."

Weiss: "Teachers are the foundation of any school. You must recognize individual strengths and use them to increase student achievement. You will have prima donnas who are excellent teachers. A good principal will work with them."

Gasparino: "Teachers are our most important resource by far. The second most is not even close. It is critical that I learn their strengths and where they will be most effective."

Fielding: "That's sort of like asking how important the sun, water and food are to sustaining life. Teachers are the most important part of a school. Without teachers who love kids and know how to deal with each child as an individual, what is the point of having school? I guess I could also put in here that I consider every grownup on campus to be a 'teacher.' All the support folks are expected to help kids when they need it. If a custodian sees a kid doing something he ought not to be doing, the custodian will talk to him about it. My secretary is a great counselor and always has a few 'adopted' kids that she talks with."

Sanders: "Each teacher needs to see him/herself as an instructional leader. They need to make decisions about the curriculum in collaboration with their colleagues and share/critique their classroom practices."

Redd: "Teachers are the main ingredient in any good school. You have to give them a little direction, and then let them go and do their thing. Encouragement is something they need a lot of, and you should find a way to see they have what they need to do their jobs right."

Question: *Best advice when dealing with teachers?*

Phipps: "Respect them. Understand their concerns. Serve them, and if they need something, get it."

Roy Miller: "They are human and make mistakes too."

Belanger: "Always remember to communicate with them often, make them feel special, have high expectations and most of all be fair and consistent."

Mitchell: "Remember that teachers are individuals with lives outside of school. Before labeling a teacher as a 'bad' teacher, take time to talk about non-school issues in a non-threatening environment — during class change, parking lot, sitting near them at a school function. Ask about their family, vacation spots, hobbies, etc. Just get personal to get professional. From building trust, you can gain entry into their classroom or hearts without being perceived as a threat. Very important — let them know that you understand 'family first' — if someone is ill, or they need to take time off for a teacher conference or doctor's appointment for their child – support them! You will gain their loyalty big time!"

Michael Miller: "Treat them professionally and openly. No secrets. No put downs."

Graham: "Know what you believe about education and about human beings. Deal with teachers directly and professionally. Stay away from socializing with them because even if you can make the distinction between professional and personal issues, they may be unable to do so."

Pichard: "Remember how it was when you were a teacher? If you were that teacher what would you want done if you were in this situation? Sometimes reflective thinking before any 'off the cuff' decisions are made is the best advice. It is also wonderful if you have an Assistant Principal to bounce ideas off of… for another perspective."

Spano: "Make them feel appreciated and listened to."

Weiss: "Listen to concerns and do not feel obligated to make decisions immediately before understanding the impact on others."

Gasparino: "The best advice I have for dealing with teachers is to realize that the overwhelming majority care and want to do the best they can. Treat them with professionalism and respect."

Fielding: "I'm not sure what the question is after, but the Golden Rule would probably be a good answer, treat them the same way you would want to be treated. I guess our HR department would also tell principals to be careful, particularly when dealing with a contract issue or potential grievance. I've never had the experience, but the HR people talk about a teacher flat out lying about something a principal told them. Maybe I'm naive, but I think if you've built a relationship with the teacher, that won't be a problem and so far that has worked. Yes, there are times when you have to be tough and tell teachers things they don't want to hear. Tell the truth, the whole truth and nothing but the truth."

Sanders: "Teachers really value autonomy; they need to be included in the decision-making process especially over those areas that most affect them. Teachers thrive on teams; get them working together."

Redd: "Listen to them and look them in the eye while your listening. Ingest what they have said and give your interpretation back."

Question: *Best advice for dealing with conflict?*

Phipps: "Listen. Don't make rash judgments. If you need a day to think about it, take a day. And whatever decision you make, make it a win-win situation."

Roy Miller: "Upfront and 'shoot from the hip.' I have my conferences, but they aren't long and (are) very much to the point. Allow teachers 'due process.' "

Belanger: "Meet with people face to face and listen carefully to what they have to say. Always go for the win/win scenario and always have them leave feeling like to care."

Mitchell: "If you are in the middle of the conflict, remember that you have two ears and one mouth; in other words, listen more than you talk. Also, there is more to gain if you admit that you have some responsibility in building the conflict. If you are trying to mediate a conflict, place yourself in the middle, give each side time to speak (one side speaking at a time), ask each what it is they want resolved, how can everyone make it happen — go for win-win or close to win-win."

Michael Miller: "Calmly and directly. When it happens."

Graham: "Data, documentation, direct communication."

Pichard: "This may not be the best advice... but it was a final strategy of dealing with two staff members who were at each other constantly. I called them into my office, got them focused on what we were going to discuss. Then I said, 'I am going to lunch duty now. When I come back to my office I hope you two will have this worked out before I get back. The only way you two can leave is if you settle this today. When I come back... if you are still here we will continue to talk. If one of you is still here then I guess we only have a one sided issue that you can't get over. If of you are gone... then this issue is settled and all of us can move on.' When I came back from lunch no one was in my office and I had a note from both staff members signed saying — 'ALL IS WELL!' "

Spano: "Be sure you have all your eggs in the basket before moving forward."

Weiss: "Conflict is usually caused by poor communication. Bring parties together to resolve conflict."

Gasparino: "The best advice for dealing with conflict is to realize that you cannot avoid it. It is our job to resolve conflict with compassion, sensitivity, and intelligence. Often times, conflict can lead to growth for all involved (at least, that's what you should hope for)."

Fielding: "Conflict, unfortunately, seems to be inevitable in this job. If it is with kids, the rule is 'you tell me your side and the other doesn't interrupt, then we switch and if the stories match, we figure out what to do to fix it and go back to work. If the stories don't match, we start over until they do.' (That comes across much more clear in real conversation.) If the conflict is with grownups, just remember that the madder they are, the calmer you have to be. Of course the best advice is to try to find ways to avoid conflict if at all possible.

Sanders: "Always try to include all parties in the resolution process. Be straightforward."

Redd: "Make sure you hear both sides of a situation, and make a decision. If you are not sure what to do get some advice from the higher ups!"

Question: *Looking back, what was the hardest, or easiest, challenge to overcome due to the previous principal of your school?*

Phipps: "The previous principal was there so long, and the staff had been with him a long time. If you make changes they say, 'We used to do it this way.' You have to try to get people to share your vision. You have to win them. Change scares people. If he (previous principal) was good — now it is new — and it is harder to win them and get them to trust you."

Roy Miller: "Hardest — Accountability!"

Belanger: "The hardest was working to get out of debt in our internal budget as well as with our School Advisory Board budget. The easiest challenge was making sure the grounds looked good. That was the previous principal's pet peeve and the campus was well groomed."

Mitchell: "The most difficult challenge was to overcome the perception that a female could not do the job. At 5 feet 4 inches I hardly matched the towering 6 foot plus stature and the perception that I could not handle a school so large with so many 'issues.' I am a tough cookie from Brooklyn, New York, and grew up with five other siblings."

Michael Miller: "The person before me had to make ALL the decisions. I had to teach my faculty how to make decisions."

Graham: "In one school it was helping the kids understand that they were no longer in charge. In another school it was helping the adults understand that children deserve to be treated with respect. In one school it was redirecting the focus on instruction rather than athletics and/or tradition. And, in yet another (I've been moved from place to place because of needs) it was helping teachers understand that when they fight against the bigger organization (the school system) they are ultimately beating up themselves."

Pichard: "When I went to my first school the easiest challenge was that I was visible. The previous principal was not out-and-about at duty, lunch duty, walking the halls, visiting the classrooms. Teachers, children and parents started noticing this right away and I have kept this strategy at my new school that I have just opened. YOU MUST BE VISIBLE. The hardest thing is always the saying, 'This is how it has been done before' and as a new principal you must be ready to expect this. Teachers are NOT creatures of habit. They really do not like change... maybe a small percentage... but most folks like things in a nice box tied in a red bow... just like it has been before. So as a new principal get ready for this one."

Spano: "I have been in six different schools and each one had it own unique challenges. Just be cautious before making changes. Get a lay of the land first."

Weiss: "The principal before me had a laissez faire attitude toward staff professional policies such as being to work on time, sick leave, panning etc. When I became principal it was apparent that I had to develop a staff handbook which outlined professional practices for teachers and staff."

Gasparino: "The reason I was appointed principal at my current school was that my predecessor allowed the school to become divided. Teachers, parents, and the PTO sided either for or against her. It became so bad that there were demonstrations and people wore different colored ribbons to indicate their allegiance. The school had gone through three different principals in seven years. It was my job to unite the school community. I am finishing my fifth year there now and will be returning next year."

Fielding: "That one is easy; I followed the same principal twice. He was never available, never told anybody where he was going and wasn't a people person. All I had to do was make sure the door is open, everybody knows where I am, and listen. In my first school, the secretary, data base manager and bookkeeper were all the same person, and she was the wife of a previous principal who had retired. The guy who was principal before me didn't like her and consequently didn't tell her anything. After I figured out her relationship to him, I told her that I'd always tell her where I was, I would never ask her to lie about it to protect me, and if she got frustrated with something, anything, anybody, to come in close the door and kick, scream, cuss, throw things, whatever she wanted and when she finishes, she leaves and I forget it. Actually, I now tell the whole staff that; their spouse or pet doesn't get paid to listen to it. When I got to my second school following him, it was one week before teachers came back and the school had a terrible reputation around the district as being unfriendly. In fact, as they told me after my first couple of months, they were called 'Idylwild, where the teachers are idle and the kids are wild.' At my first faculty meeting, the first time I had met most of them, I said 'that #%$*& will change whether I'm here six weeks or twenty years.' Next year will be number twenty and we enjoy a great reputation.

Sanders: "Changing the culture of the adults in the school. Typically, the principal will dictate the school's culture and that is the hardest single area to change."

Redd: "The previous principal was the principal when I was a student in this building. I think he was a veteran that did a very good job."

Question: *What has been the most rewarding part of your years as a principal?*

Phipps: "Having staff members who do not want to leave. Some numbers (of teachers) went down after I started the position as principal, but they had to leave, even though they did all they could to stay. Seeing smiles on the staff's faces, that's rewarding."

Roy Miller: "Students' Success."

Belanger: "Being able to develop goals and design strategies to meet those goals. It is very rewarding to have a vision for your school, making it known to all the stakeholders and having everyone, parents, students and staff work together to accomplish your goals."

Mitchell: "Helping students realize some level of success for the first time. As an example, I worked with a student who was an underachiever — academically and behaviorally. He was failing all of his subjects, had scored at the lowest level on standardized tests, and had very low self-esteem. I taught him a reading strategy and asked him to research the strategy — teach it to others during his lunch time, and then prepare a powerpoint to present to teachers during a faculty meeting. He went for broke — scored at or above grade level on all of the standardized tests in the eighth grade, passed eighth grade, and surprised me with a note in the yearbook that stated that he was most thankful for that experience! Students who show progress and reach a level of success that they did not have before are the most rewarding experiences any principal could have."

Michael Miller: "See how much my teachers have grown and seeing such a rise in student performance. I was able to take a school everyone in the district made fun of to one where over 20 schools from around the state came to visit last year. I believe my job is to make a teacher be the best they can be and I am constantly amazed at how far my teachers have come. There is nothing they can't accomplish."

Graham: "Experiencing the joy of watching high school seniors go from knowing 'everything' to wanting to know anything we'll share as they are ready (or not) to walk out the door. As I continue in my career, I find a lot of satisfaction in having a part in mentoring/training administrators who aspire to become principals."

Pichard: "There have been many rewarding experiences but I would say it is when I see students, parents or community members out and they have a nice comment about the school, my teacher or teachers or sometimes even myself. These comments make it easier to get up the next day to go to work knowing that to someone you made a difference."

Spano: "When I see a child be successful and know that my staff enjoys coming to work each day."

Weiss: "Two things, a) the teachers that I have been able to develop into outstanding professionals, and b) seeing students improve their behavior and academics when most people had given up on them."

Gasparino: "My most rewarding experience was when our school became a Title I Choice school whereby parents from failing schools could opt to send their children to us. There were may that feared that this would result in a decline in our academic achievement. Instead our test scores went up and two years later, we were recognized as the 15th top performing elementary school in the state of Florida."

Fielding: "Seeing teachers and kids grow and learn. Of course there are a million stories about this."

Sanders: "Creating a school climate that is warm and caring for all students, but still maintains high expectations for their ability to perform high level tasks."

Redd: "The kids have been the most fun through the years. I get a new batch of them every year, and I get to meet so many kids that are nice people."

Question: *It has been noted that the schools are constantly being watched by groups and politicians for their own beneficial reasons. A few of these people are legislators and the media. Please give your advice, or an analogy, on this constant surveillance for personal gain.*

Phipps: "I remember doing a presentation for a Kiwanis group and they wanted to know what is going on with education due to the bad news all the media was portraying. I told him, 'Come on out to the school and spend a day in a classroom. You will see what teachers go through daily.' I did have a few spend the day, and after that they understood. They saw the teacher deal with all the different personalities, different levels of learning, different chains of instruction, the testing, how the teacher would have kids on the computer, kids reading, and the list goes on. The newspapers have to sell — they have to have drama. Have an open door policy. Invite people to come in and see what is going on."

Roy Miller: "I always assume that 'Big Brother' is watching. However, if news can't be found, it is sometimes made."

Belanger: "Schools, especially public schools are constantly under the microscope. Law makers often use data in a way that is not always comprehensible to schools personnel, but it may be to the general public, especially during an election year. In our area, we have a large population of retirees who are always looking for ways to cut taxes, and often lowering school taxes is something that gets votes. Most of us wish we could make the retirees understand that if you don't pay for education first, you will pay for it later, with building more prisons."

Mitchell: "If politicians and the media shared their surveillance expertise with students, imagine the benefits students would gain from constantly watching what goes on in school?"

Michael Miller: "My goal is to always be transparent to what we are doing. That takes a lot of speculating away from the media."

Graham: "I'll focus on the media as the politicians are a temporary entity at any given time… it's important to know who is who but it is probably unhealthy to take any of them too seriously. The responsible thing to do is know them, inform them and stays informed about them, and vote intelligently. As far as the media: You owe them nothing. While there is value in having a relationship with someone who has a lot more ink than you, avoid being pushed and/or bullied by them. I have 'grounded' reporters from my campus. At the same time, I try to cultivate a relationship so when the 'bad' story occurs (and it will); there may be some hope of your version being accurate because of the time spent during the 'good' stories. The story will be written regardless, so when you can give your side it is good to have someone you've forged some sort of relationship with to hear it."

Pichard: "Schools are the scapegoat of society. Whenever there is a new program… let's put it in the schools. Gun Control, Bullying, Sexual Harassment, Character Education Poster Contests, etc… everyone uses the schools as their own training area. Even the local politicians, police, fire, environmental groups, civic organizations all have a school component of essay, poetry, poster, banner, public speaking, etc... to get the schools involved in their effort or organization. Schools and the districts need to do a better job of screening all these requests so the teachers can do their job in teaching the students. Yes, many of these are very important causes but so many of them are time consuming and are very poorly organized which is frustrating to the teaching staff, students and parents."

Spano: " Politicians, newspapers, upset parents, etc., will all keep a close eye on you. My best advice is to stay below the radar!!!!"

Weiss: "Have an open door policy for yourself and for the school. Invite politicians, the media, and parents to spend time at the school to observe first hand the challenges educators face everyday. This will usually diffuse critics once they see first hand what educators contend with on a daily basis."

Gasparino: "As for the media, they will be on the phone wanting to visit our school if there is a problem, perceived on not. Just this year, we have what we call a 'fall festival' party (we can't call it Halloween). A parent called the next day saying that she saw on the news that a certain kind of candy had been recalled because of having found metal shards in one lollipop. To be on the safe side, we contacted our parents on this. Somehow the media found out, and by that afternoon I was on the phone fielding calls from the media and they parked outside the school trying to interview parents.

"As for legislators, it seems that they are very fond of passing unfunded mandates and adding things to an already full school day."

Fielding: "Well, this is sort of like my answer to #2. I believe that much of my job is keeping that sort of stuff as far from my teachers as I can. I tell the teachers that I'll try to keep it away from them, and if they hear some sort of rumor, please ask me before they believe it. If the teachers do the best job they can with every kid every day, what can the outside folks say that should bother us? Again, this is only possible with a supportive Board and superintendent.

"Unfortunately, at least for me, good media coverage is now considered a good thing. I was raised under a superintendent who said 'stay out of the media, good or bad, at all costs' and I tend to believe that. On occasion I've had to deal with them and I usually do it in the same sort of honest conversational manner in which this is written. I could tell you a couple of really funny stories about that too.

"One of the interviews that our district uses to hire principals lists one of the 'talents' a principal should have as 'ego drive'; I don't have any. In one of your emails you said that I'd get credit for what happens at my school whether I want it or not, and, of course, you're right. If anything not positive happens, I'll be happy to take the credit (heat) whichever, but if it's good, I'd rather the teachers get it."

Sanders: "Personally, I believe the public school system is the best chance we have for providing all children with the opportunity to be successful in life. Unfortunately, this does not seem to motivate either politicians or the media."

Redd: "Politicians want to be the watchdogs of education, they just don't want to take the blame when the proper funding isn't there."

Question: *What do you think of the new mentoring programs for beginning principals?*

Phipps: "We have a very good one in place. It is good to have someone you can share insights with and discuss issues, someone you can trust."

Roy Miller: "I'm not up to date on the program. However, I'm told that it is a good thing for those coming into the profession. Anything concerning preparation can't hurt."

Belanger: "I think they are an excellent way to support that new principal in a way that no other program can. The program is only as good as the district sees it as being important and the people involved as mentors."

Mitchell: "If it involves real on the job training without fear of failure, then I think any program that embraces that concept is an improvement."

Michael Miller: "The one in Brevard is great. I am a mentor for an Assistant Principal every year."

Graham: "I think it is too soon to tell if they will make the impact folks hope they make. I am a certified principal mentor, and I think I'll be doing things very similarly to what I've been doing for many years. Time will tell of the impact made. I do believe every beginning principal needs a mentor to turn to… so many things that only experience provides!"

Pichard: "Wonderful — I participated in one when I was an Assistant Principal. I have been a mentor principal for a number of assistant principals who are now principals, and are currently serving on my Assistant Principal's team so she can be promoted to a principal in the coming years."

Spano: "Not familiar with them."

Weiss: "The programs can be very helpful in preparing new principals. Internships as assistant principals do a good job of preparing principals with a good role model."

Gasparino: "When I became a principal, I was very fortunate in having worked for excellent administrators who helped me. This was a very informal arrangement. New mentoring programs are valuable and needed. I have been trained a mentor principal by the National Association of Elementary Principals (NAESP)."

Fielding: "I guess that depends on the mentoring program. There are a lot of consultants out there who want to train us on how to be mentors, and I'm sure some of them are good. We actually had this discussion with principals not too long ago (we need some new principals to replace us old folks) and every one of us could name a person who had been our 'mentor' at some time or other. None of them were the formal mentor assigned by the district. Mine is the lady I mentioned who now lives in Columbus. I could talk about her and her influence for a long time. What she saw in me in my 'spoiled brat' days I couldn't tell you, but here I am."

Sanders: "I think mentoring programs for new principals can be very helpful, as long as they don't require additional, nonessential work. However, I believe the most important alliance for the new principal consists of the leadership team at the school. This would probably include assistant principals, deans, counselors, etc. who would work as a collaborative team with the new principal."

Redd: "Too exhaustive and much to much red tape even to get certified."

Question: *What advice would you give a first year principal in the hiring of teachers?*

Phipps: "Go with your gut feeling."

Roy Miller: "Lean on those who have been doing it for some time. A new principal needs to realize that it is OK not to know everything your first few years."

Belanger: "Hire people who are enthusiastic about kids and have a willingness to learn."

Mitchell: "If you are unfamiliar with the teachers on your staff, make sure that you look for someone who is very much like you were as a teacher. At least you would have a friend. More seriously, you need to get a cadre of teachers that you respect and trust to informally interview the candidate — if possible, let the candidate sit in a class to watch a teacher teaching, interact with students, etc. You can then have the cadre ask what he/she would have done differently, or ask about his/her perception about what was going on, etc. In my experience, candidates have access to sample teacher interview questions from the internet or from a class. They then rehearse answers and are well prepared with 'pat' answers. You can tell more about a person's body language and how they would react to a student or situation if you put that person in 'real time.' "

Michael Miller: "Versatility and loyalty are a must."

Graham: "Never settle… avoid panic."

Pichard: "Most important or one of the most important jobs you will do for your school. A great teacher will let you sleep at night, handle parents, get along with students and other staff. A poor teacher will drive you crazy, have you in a lot of conferences with parents, staff will 'roll their eyes' when they walk by... knowing you hired this person... and often the students will be your first hint that there is a problem because they will tell you like it is in no uncertain terms, especially the older students."

Spano: "Use a committee to do all staff hiring. This way you are getting the buy-in of staff members that will be working with each hire,"

Weiss: "Do your homework. Check out the applicants references in great detail. An interview is the worst predictor of job performance."

Gasparino: "Hiring teachers is the most important thing you'll do. Always be sure to call all references and ask probing questions."

Fielding: "This is the question that caused me to write you about your survey in the first place, and people around here would tell you that this is one thing I'm passionate about. I believe that hiring teachers (and other staff) is the single most important job that a principal does. It is important to know what you want, what kind of questions will help you sort the applicants into those you want and those you don't, and understand the concept of how they 'fit' with the other teachers and staff at your school. And, I think I've said before, the best advice I ever got was 'never hire anybody dumber than you are.' Of course I didn't really understand that until I'd been a principal for about ten years.

"Some where around 23 years ago we had a superintendent who was friends with a guy who started a company which developed interviews designed to find who would be the top two or three percent in whatever field the interview was for. I could go into a long speech about how they did this, but I'm not sure how since the company was bought by a larger company and the original interviews no longer exist in that form except with some of us old folks. (I'd be happy to talk to you about that.) Anyway, at that time, and for the next seven years or so, all our building administrators were required to become trained and certified in this interview and all teacher applicants were required to take it. I am the only one left who still uses it, but I won't hire a teacher without it. You might ask why I feel that strongly about it. I believe that the interview has questions which help me sort applicants into the very top, the good ones, and those for whom I would recommend a different line of work. The company used to train us that 'it is an understanding, not a score' and I firmly believe they knew what they were talking about. You don't really have to take my word for it as most of my staff complement me on making 'good hires.' Unfortunately, I think, the company which now has control over the next generation of this interview, is quite interested in making money rather than in helping us find the best teachers. Of course, that's only my opinion, not theirs.

"In any case, my advice would be to try and find teachers who first love kids. It helps if they can see individual differences in kids and know how to individualize for those differences. We can teach them most of the rest of it. I could go on and on, but that's probably enough."

Sanders: "More important than knowledge of a subject, is the ability to develop healthy relationships with students and fellow teachers."

Redd: "Look for a little bit of experience, their ability to get along with other people and have some compassion."

Question: *What advice would you give a first year principal in the firing of teachers?*

Phipps: "Make sure you have every (bit of) evidence you need, and you are convinced this person is bad for children. This is a person's livelihood. Do not try to get rid of a teacher just because you saw them sitting at the computer one time or because they disagreed with you. Be sure it is not personal issues."

Roy Miller: "I don't have the authority to 'fire' a teacher. However, I can recommend a 'non-renewal.' With that said, you need to work very closely with the teacher in question and keep HR abreast of the situation. If tenured, it takes a lot of documentation to remove a teacher."

Belanger: "Do it as soon as you can, the longer you wait the more difficult it is for you, the teacher and your staff. Don't be afraid that it will take too much time because a poor teacher is poison to your organization and to the reputation of your entire staff."

Mitchell: "Make sure that you have all of your ducks in a row. Know the rules. I had to have a teacher fired for being under the influence of alcohol. I had suspicions, but was always one duck out of line. I was able to align my ducks, and after four years of worrying, I was able to get him out of my school."

Michael Miller: "It is probably the hardest thing you have to do but you have to ask yourself the question of whether or not you would want your own child in that room. If the answer is no, then you have no choice."

Graham: "Never settle. Avoid panic. Document, document, document. (Would you want this teacher for your own child?)"

Pichard: "Document, document, document. Have your 'ducks' in a row. Also never meet with a teacher by yourself... have another administrator in the meeting with you. Keep your Area Superintendent, District Labor Relations or Human Resources Department informed of all the things that you are doing because they may some information that you have not thought about in pursuing this matter. This is also a time when a fellow principal that you respect and trust can also be a good sounding board for you."

Spano: "Be sure to document, try to assist this person before considering firing."

Weiss: "Follow procedures and consult with central office personnel. The actual firing of a teacher is usually a long process which requires tenacity and knowledge of the law by the administration."

Gasparino: "Firing teachers is a difficult process. It is best to terminate their employment when they are still on annual contract. If you are going to fire a teacher, work closely with your supervisor and Human Resources office. You need to have well-developed documentation and patience."

Fielding: "Do (the hiring) well and you won't have to."

"Okay, sometimes you inherit a problem or get a 'gift' from personnel that somebody else can't handle and you have to think about firing. It's always better if you can find SOMETHING, ANYTHING, that they are good at and redirect them, but if not, just be careful and follow the rules. This is one area where you should ask for help and make sure to dot the 'Is' and cross the 'Ts.'"

Sanders: "Try to be out in classrooms as much as possible to develop an in-depth understanding of each teacher's level of effectiveness. Ineffective teachers should be trained to become effective or replaced."

Redd: "Document, document, document. Meet, offer suggestions, and document some more."

Question: *Name the three most important things you feel should be changed in the educational system of our country?*

Phipps: "Testing — there is too much — too much stress. Accountable is fine, but the testing is too much. We have two weeks of testing. They should cut it back and let us teach, especially in elementary. Let them be children. The children need to learn to play, to socialize. Corporations put people in cubicles take the cubicles away and you get cooperative teaming."

Roy Miller: "Remove tenure. Site base management. More freedom to align curriculum with needs of school."

Belanger: "1.) High stakes testing that involve punishing students and schools.

"2.) Funding for schools, every school population is unique and we must meet the individual needs of our students first. This is especially true of our ESE populations.

"3.) Teacher unions who support the weakest and poorest teachers."

Mitchell: "Pay for teachers needs to be on par with other professionals that we entrust our most precious national resource — children. It is difficult to reconcile the notion that teachers continue to go into teaching for the love of it when they have families to support and gas prices are reaching four dollars a gallon.

"Eliminate any merit pay system for teachers. Children are not cars, real estate, or stocks. We should not be paid 'extra' for helping kids realize success. That is why we get paid in the first place. Raise salaries and we would attract the best individuals and more importantly, keep them.

"Eliminate tenure. Have you ever seen the work ethic, loyalty, and care leave so fast in some individuals when they get 'tenured?' The teachers' union becomes their passion, and the administration their target. Students become a distant memory."

Michael Miller: "Testing pressures, low regard of teachers, and the feeling that every school should look and produce the same."

Graham: "University teaching preparation has failed to keep up with the needs of public schools. Lip service of legislators needs to become action re: the importance/value of educators. Valid/researched/real-life data needs to drive decisions."

Pichard: "RESPECT: (intrinsic) I tell my teachers that parents and community members have high expectations of school employees (teacher, administrator or support staff). In order to be respected you must earn respect. We have not done a great job in the arena because we often do not communicate with parents when needed or some of our fellow professionals commit some type of crime that mares our entire profession. Then everyone dumps us into the same basket with 'all the bad apples.' I think this is why many folks are looking to other types of schooling. We will always have these folks in our profession, but we need to celebrate and let our communities know the school system is the greatest in the world.

"LUNCH FUNDING: I think we should give all students a free lunch also. My school provides a free breakfast to any student who wants it. I realize it would cost the government some money, but the ones who suffer are the middle to lower income families that do not qualify for Free and Reduced Lunch. Many a teacher and I have paid for or loaned money to students so they would not go hungry during the day. Students get upset in the morning when they have forgotten their lunch money and know they are not going to get anything to eat. Even though we have a system in place to prevent this at my school they still feel upset. If the legislatures want to discuss a break for families this may be a start.

"ACCOUNTABILTY: I am all for accountability of my students, staff, etc. However, the 'A' word has taken on a whole new profile. Legislators and State Boards of Education and the US Congress are making the rules and guidelines but many of neither them, nor their staffers have been in a school to even see what goes on each day. "NO CHILD LEFT BEHIND has not only left children behind but also has left teachers, administrators, support staff, parents and communities behind. The program makes good press but when money is not linked with legislation to impact a program then the program needs to be placed on the back burner until funding can fully support this program for a ten to twenty year period, with increases in the funding as more students and staff enter that school.

"Florida has a grading system which is based on our Florida Comprehensive Achievement Testing (FCAT). There is a lot of pressure on students, teachers of those grade levels being tested, the rest of the school staff to perform so that their school can be an 'A' school. It is a 'crap shoot' when you are hoping and praying that the students in your school who are taking the test will do their best and work hard on the battery of tests. They can score an 'A' grade and your school looks wonderful and you get perks such as A + Bonus Recognition Money, letters for community leaders and politicians congratulating you on a fine job and press releases by the district. Or you can be a 'B or lower school' and see your name constantly in the press whenever there is an article about low achieving schools (schools not making an A), required training for your school since you did not make an 'A' and just the stigma and questioning of why did we score what we did.

"We have to remember that we are not manufacturing 'Widgets'"that can be patterned, molded and colored so they all come out the same. We are working with students who come to school from very caring homes to students who get themselves up each morning get dressed and catch the bus while parents (if they are living with them) are still sleeping. We have children that are running from a parent while the other parent moves the children from one location to another preventing another beating or abusive situation. We have parents who think school is a good place for daycare while they go work. As long as the school does not call they are fine.

"So as we look at Accountability we must be serious on how to help our students rather than just dumping us into a program or program title which has no backing or support."

Spano: "The grading of schools. Funding of schools. Providing more alternative placements for kids that are a constant disruption to the educational setting. It should be a privilege to attend a school and if you abuse that privilege then an alternative setting should be provided."

Weiss: "1) School Grading Policies — School grading policies are unfair in most cases. For the most part, low performing schools have very low parent involvement, students who live at the lower end of the socioeconomic scale and live in single parent homes. The deck is stacked against these schools.

"2) Teacher Tenure and Retention Practices — In order to increase salaries teacher tenure practices and how teachers are paid will have to be revised. First of all, every tenured teacher should have a thorough evaluation every three to five years to determine if their contract should be renewed. In most cases gain scores and other measures that determine student growth would be evaluated. If science and math teachers are in demand we should pay them more. Most teacher salary schedules now are based on years of experience and degree and not anything else. We need different salary schedules for teachers depending on what they teach.

"3) Title I and IDEA — There is too much paperwork and government intrusion with these two programs.

"4) No Child Left Behind — This act is far too punitive and punishes educators for variables they can not control related to student achievement. I have no problems with educators being held accountable for student performance. However, the playing field is not level in terms of socio-economic status, student transience and support for education by parents."

Gasparino: "One thing that should be changed is the way we evaluate schools. Accountability is important and necessary. However, it should be based on more than one test score. Another is funding for schools. Public money should not be diverted to private schools. Lastly, we have to do a better job in reclaiming public trust."

Fielding: "Did you forget? I try to stay away from politics........... yeah, I know, it's impossible. The country is a big place with lots of different needs and ways of doing things; I can barely keep up with the nonsense in Florida. In general, I think we are placing way too much emphasis on high stakes tests. I don't mind being accountable for student growth and some of the testing which has been implemented in the last several years has actually been beneficial and improved teaching and learning. But, we have also made a bunch of kids and grownups a bit neurotic with the pressure."

Sanders: "The curriculum needs to reflect the knowledge and skills that are required by the 21st Century global economy. We need to increase the depth of understanding rather than 'covering' material. We need to help students see the connections between big ideas and bodies of knowledge rather than teaching isolated disciplines. Instruction should aim for authentic tasks in real world settings."

Redd: "Less emphasis on testing. Mandated financing."

Question: *How would you advise a first year principal in regard to standardized testing?*

Phipps: "Do not play it up. That is too much pressure on the kids and parents. Teach the standards and curriculum and all will be fine."

Roy Miller: "Teach the standards (state and local). Make sure your faculty knows what is expected of them. Continue to review the data and look for ways to improve non-proficient. "

Belanger: "Make sure your teachers understand the standards that are to be testing and meet with them frequently to monitor progress. Support standardized testing even though you may not always agree with it."

Mitchell: "Be positive about it. Do not get hung up in the drama. Use the data to drive your school's curriculum – stay focused on the kids!"

Michael Miller: "Look at your past data. Let the data drive your instruction."

Graham: "Forget the test, focus on the standards, be willing to be accountable and hold the same level for your teachers."

Pichard: "I would tell a first year principal that standardized testing is a very serious issue. There are a lot of ramifications if it is not done correctly due to test security items."

Spano: "Know your data. Train your teachers and prepare your students."

Weiss: "Give teachers in-service on administration and interpretation of tests to ensure validity and reliability. Make sure special education teachers review IEPs for accommodations."

Gasparino: "Whether we like it or not, standardized testing is the way our schools are judged. First year principals need to become proficient in analyzing student performance data and use it to improve instructional programs."

Fielding: "Short answer.........hire the best teachers, give them what they need and the testing will take care of itself. Making yourself or your teachers stressed over standardized test results won't make them better."

Sanders: "It is extremely important that all teachers have their curriculum aligned to the standards that are being assessed. Instructional calendars and curriculum mapping are essential."

Redd: "Make sure your teachers have all the review materials they need, and make sure they are using it."

Question: *How would you measure your success as a principal?*

Phipps: "By the smiles on the kid's faces, by knowing they want to come to school, and by teacher retention, the staff wanting to come to work. We (principals) have to remember our staff has family. I tell them, Go home be with your family. Family comes first. The job will be here. If something happens to you and me, they will replace us. When all else fails, family is who will be there and who you need."

Roy Miller: "The satisfaction of the teachers and parents gauge my success and/or failure. My evaluations are exemplary; however, to me the people I serve are my number one concern."

Belanger: "By the success of goals met with students, teachers and the community. If your school is a place where the community wants to gather, you have success."

Mitchell: "I have had some major obstacles — first female in a school with a history that goes back to the '60's — African American within a white majority community — 'good ol' boy' mindsets. How do I measure my success? I am still healthy! I have increased all-around student achievement, increased National Board Certified teachers and those pursuing NBCT, we are honored as a Music Demonstration School, have an excellent Drama and Art program, pursuing International Baccalaureate Middle Years Program accreditation, and many other achievements have been realized with the support and help from a great faculty that I have built in my five years."

Michael Miller: "My test scores and the number of visitors I have each year to see how we are getting these results."

Graham: "Is a place better because I've been the leader?"

Pichard: "I have had an 'A' school for the past seven years. We moved from a 'C' school to an 'A' school. I have worked hard and my staff knows I would not ask them to do anything that I would not do. Each year the Teacher's Union does a school survey of building administrators and I have had good scores from my staff and on the Client Surveys given to parents my schools have had wonderful scores."

Spano: "Student achievement!"

Weiss: "I measure my success as a principal by student achievement and teacher performance. As a principal of a special day school that serves Emotional/Behavior Disordered students success is also measured in terms of student attendance, student behavior change and overall safety at the school."

Gasparino: "I believe that I have grown to be a successful principal. I received the Commissioner's Principal Achievement Award for Outstanding Leadership. Hopefully, that means something."

Fielding: "Are the kids learning? Is the staff happy? Do they all love kids? Do they love their jobs? Do the parents and others describe us as a friendly school? Things like that."

Sanders: "I think a principal should measure his/her success by the climate/culture that has been created. The ideal would be to have a school culture in place where all teachers and staff believe they are responsible for the learning and success of all students."

Redd: "I have had many good years I get along with students, parents, and teachers for the most part. I would say that I have been fair with my decisions."

Question: *Did you have a mentor, and if yes, could you share a story about him or her?*

Phipps: "I had two mentors: Mr. Jerry Hartwig and Mr. Jerry Primus. Mr. Hartwig taught me the ins and outs of being a principal. He got me prepared by throwing me a sack and saying, 'Here, do it.' Mr. Primus was so organized. He made me do the same be organized. He also told me, 'Every decision you make, make sure it is in the best interest of that child.' My dad used to tell me that too."

Roy Miller: The only mentor I had was after I became a principal and went through the cohort program from the state department. It wasn't as successful as I had wished. However, we both had schools and were very busy. She was there to answer questions and that meant a lot to me."

Belanger: "Yes, she was the principal in a school where I was a teacher. She saw leadership abilities in me and involved me in many experiences to widen my view of her position. She encouraged me to go to graduate school and to meet the requirements of an administrator. I was later appointed her Asst. Principal at the school. She taught me how to hire the best and the brightest of teachers, which I feel is my strongest asset."

Mitchell: "Bob Donaldson — former Area Superintendent — knew my pain, and worked with me for hours on end until I figured it out 'myself.' He would always say, 'Now you came up with that idea yourself and I think that it is pretty good!' "

Michael Miller: "My Principal and my mentor had opposite leadership styles. This allowed me to see where my style was."

Graham: "I have a fabulous mentor. When I was being moved at the direction of the superintendent from a brand new school I had opened just a year before to a school where all administrators were being removed and a team of us were going in to fix a mess (they called us the 'dream team' as if that would make us any happier about the move), my mentor called and asked if I was crying. I said, 'Of course I am.' Her response, 'Then get in the bathroom until you are finished. No one needs to see you cry. They need to see your strength and understanding that you work for an organization.' That was the end of my public tears...to this day."

Pichard: "I had two great mentors. Diane Okoniewski was my principal when I was an Assistant Principal. I was with her for six and one-half years. She and I had a great relationship. We actually use to walk when we had meetings in the evenings just to get out of the building. We would start walking down the street and parents, neighbors and students would come out and talk to us. Sometimes the students would be on their bikes riding along side of us. Had a great time. Joseph O'Brien provided me a lot of opportunities when I was teaching for him to have some administrative duties or experiences. The experiences that he provided prepared me for my AP position. He was a great cheerleader for me and my professional career."

Spano: "No."

Weiss: "Yes I had a mentor. She gave me very good advice and always told me 'there is no need to be heavy handed when dealing with people. Everyone knows you are in charge.' "

Gasparino: "I was fortunate to have worked for two administrators that helped guide me."

Fielding: "Yes, I've talked about her in other questions and probably most of my answers have some bit of her in them. A story...let's see…I could tell the one about us cleaning a whole hog in my office for a staff pig roast…or how we threw her a surprise birthday party at her house for a couple hundred of her closest friends… or…the first time I met her in a conference with the folks from DOE, it was Halloween and I was wearing a diaper…the list goes on!!! I could probably come up with a serious one if you like, but really, they are throughout my answers.

Sanders: "I did not have a mentor."

Redd: "No, don't have one."

Question: *How would you advise a first year principal in preparing for public relations?*

Phipps: "Do not always attack at the first moment you hear something negative. If you hear something negative, approach it in a positive way and be very upbeat."

Roy Miller: "Don't speak unless spoken to. When you speak, say as little as necessary to get you through the interview. Also, if you don't know the answer — say NOTHING!"

Belanger: "Be transparent; never try to hide something because it will always come out that you were not truthful. Protecting your students has to be the first priority and when it doubt about answering to the media, get guidance from someone who has been there."

Mitchell: "If you do not have a best foot to put forward, get someone else for the job! Remember that you represent more than your self. Treat others as you would like to be treated. Be wary of what is said to the media — call your district communications office when in doubt!"

Michael Miller: "Answer honestly and openly."

Graham: "Take your time, ask questions when you need to, avoid making promises you will be unable to keep, and smile a lot! (Or, 'never let them see you sweat')."

Pichard: "Be careful of the press... because what you say may not be what is printed. Always use your Public Relations Department if the school district has a contact to bounce things off of before sending any items or talking about sensitive issues."

Spano: "Be open and honest. Be careful!!!! Some reporters are just looking for a negative story. If you find someone like this then avoid them."

Weiss: "Public Relations are extremely important. Besides publishing newsletters and having parent involvement activities the principal should train staff as to the skills required in working with parents. At my school we did a book study, *Understanding Poverty* by Ruby Payne, to have a thorough understanding."

Gasparino: "A first year principal needs to recognize that public relations and the public's perception is critical to your success or failure. Be sure to get the good news out and control negative news. Remember to be sure to get the information across that you want no matter what questions may be asked. Weigh your words carefully and be a good communicator.

Fielding: "I prefer to leave that to someone on my staff who is better at it. If I have to talk with the media, I just try to be honest, never say anything I don't want to see in print or have read to me by the opposing attorney.

"These days public schools are under attack from all sorts of places and that requires us to be a bit proactive in getting out the good news. If your school has special programs or exciting things that may be out of the norm, or staff that do something outstanding, these are the things you want to share with the media. Our district has a Public Information Officer who handles that sort of stuff. In smaller districts the principal may have to do it or have someone on staff take care of it. We have a lot of business partners, and I have staff members who work with each of them."

Sanders: "Public relations are vital to the success of any change efforts, especially if the school had previously been seen in a negative light. Building programs that attract interest and marketing these successes will eventually change public perception."

Redd: "Treat people the way you want them to treat you."

Question: *Any suggestions for disciplining students?*

Phipps: "Treat them with respect. Sometimes they say, I do not know why I did it, and they really do not know."

Roy Miller: "When (a student is) corrected, also let them know you care and that you love them. Make family connections to build on the relationship. They want to know that you care, and if so, you will see them fewer times for negative behavior and more for just time to talk."

Belanger: "Give your teachers power over what happens in their classrooms. Give them steps to follow and interventions to give before the administration gets involved. Train teachers to be good at disciplining their own students. When it is necessary for the administration must get involved, don't get angry or 'even.' State the policies and procedures and follow through with them equally with every student."

Mitchell: "Dignity. Do not take it away from them. No matter what the student did, he/she knows that his authority is less than yours. He knows that he has little or no power. A student and his/her parent will be more accepting of the discipline consequences and more sorrowful for and reflective of the misbehavior if the student can walk out of the school without shame."

Michael Miller: "Consistency and fairly."

Graham: "Be sure students know the expectations and then be sure to dole out the consequences promised. Kids want to know what is expected of them… and they really want (and need) parameters in spite of their objections to the contrary."

Pichard: "Make sure you always have the entire story before proceeding with any discipline. Sometimes things are cut and dry especially if you are part of it. It gets really sticky when others are involved… even teachers and then convey that they really didn't see it. This is the hard part to piece the puzzle together. We do not have a crystal ball so we have to rely on witnesses, perceptions and hopefully some integrity and honesty when working with students. Then when you think you have the entire story you have to look at the 'puzzle' and see what the picture really looks like. Sometimes it comes together quite nicely and it is clear and concise. Other times it looks like some old 'puzzle' that has a few pieces missing and you will never find them. Discipline is probably one of the hardest things to do because you have the final word on whether a student stays in school, suspended or expelled. Discipline or should I say good discipline involves counseling and time. The time spent today with a student or group of students may limit the time you have to spend with them in the future about the same issue or situation. Discipline is most looked on as a punitive exercise, but this is where you have to be a leader so that students, parents and teachers will know you are fair in your decisions. Every disciplinary action does not need a consequence after you have investigated thoroughly. Parents are the toughest part of the 'discipline wheel.' They want to 'spin' that their child does not lie, would not do this or that. They want justice and to make sure that all the students are getting the same punishment. This is where the 'counseling' comes into play. It is easier to say to a parent that Johnny told me that he hit so and so, or that they took the chips from the cafeteria because they were hungry. Discipline… probably the most time consuming and worst aspect of the job… especially when there is a FULL MOON."

Spano: "Students must understand that the classroom is not a place to disrupt. Very simply stated, 'Teachers have a right to teach and students have a right to learn.' "

Weiss: "In my 20 years as principal of a special day school in my work with students with emotional problems/behavior I have learned a great deal about discipline. First of all, suspending students to change behavior does not work. The teachers with the fewest discipline problems connect with students."

Gasparino: "Being fair when disciplining a student does not always mean treating everyone the same. If it is a minor incident, deal with it and get them back to class. Usually, these are the students who can least afford to miss instruction. Inform parents when appropriate. Don't let anyone intimidate others. No one should be afraid to be in school. Follow district guidelines and consult with your supervisor when in doubt."

Fielding: "There was a little bit of this in the question on conflict. Probably the shortest and best advice would be to consider how you would want it handled if your own child was in the situation."

Sanders: "Schools should try to change negative behavior through progressive disciplinary actions. A school wide plan should be developed by a representative group. All staff and students should be trained."

Redd: "Question everyone you can before making a decision. Don't be as rough on them the first time. If they mess up again, more and stiffer punishment."

Question: *Share the most humorous experience you've had as a principal.*

Phipps: "I was observing a 2nd grade teacher and after she told the kids to get ready for lunch, I pulled my money out of my pocket. My money was a bunch of ones so it looked like a lot. One of the kids said, 'Wow! You have a lot of money! Where do you work?' "

Then there was the group of boys I used to talk to about how to speak to people, how to say hello and be polite. These students were coming down the hall one day and I walked right by them. I realized I did not say hello and neither did they, so I stopped, went back and asked, What do I say to you each morning? They all three said, 'Stop running.' "

Roy Miller: "Sitting with the faculty over the summer at a week long art integration intensive and going together to watch 'Chicago' live. It was very embarrassing sitting on the front row and watching some of the scenes together."

Belanger: "I am not sure how humorous this is, but it certainly was a first for me. I had hired a new Reading Coach who was a veteran teacher and who also had her degree in Ed. Leadership.(Just when you think someone has the 'big picture', they don't!) After a week long of testing students, the Reading Coach wanted to thank the teachers and assistants who had helped in the testing. She made a 'goodie bag for each staff member and put the bag in each of their mailboxes. The problem was that each bag contained a bottle of Khalua, an alcoholic drink. When I questioned her reasoning for bringing alcoholic beverages on campus and then presenting them to staff her answer was, 'Well, they sold it at the local grocery store so I thought it was O.K.' My comment was, 'They also sell condoms, but I would hope you wouldn't pass those out either.' Needless to say the Reading Coach is no longer employed here, but that experience certainly brings a lot of laughs when we re-visit a 'what were they thinking' experience."

Mitchell: "I was at the beauty salon one Saturday morning when my stylist asked me if I knew a parent that was one of her clients. I told the stylist that I had met so many parents, but since it was my first month at the school, had not had the opportunity to develop many relationships with students or parents. She then informed me that I needed to 'be aware' of a parent that was talking badly about me, wishing that the former principal was still there, and that I came from 'nowhere.' The parent was also upset because I decided that not allowing more girls on the school's dance team was unfair to students who could not afford the costumes and uniforms, and were coming from out of county or out of state schools (they were not at the school the previous year, so they could not attend the tryout — and besides — there is enough competition on the high school level!). The stylist, who has a personality like Queen Latifah, allowed the parent to ramble on for several minutes before she asked, 'Have you ever talked to Mrs. Mitchell?' The parent replied, 'I wouldn't waste time with that witch.' The stylist then said — 'Do you know that Mrs. Mitchell has been a client of mine for seven years? — I suggest that you talk with her — you will be surprised…etc.' About mid-September, I was told by my secretary that a parent in the front office wanted to see me — it was the parent the stylist was talking about. She had a great big plant for my office, and a note welcoming me to the school, and thanking me for talking to her daughter in the cafeteria. I graciously thanked her and hid the fact that I did not remember any special conversation with a student (I talk to many students during lunch duty). From that day forward, on every holiday, I received enough plants and flowers to fill a small garden. I did not have the heart to say that she did not have to continue — I am sure that it was doing wonders for her conscience (I soon discovered who her daughter was — one with few friends, on most days looked aimlessly for a welcoming face amongst her peers in the cafeteria — and the kind of kid I zoom in on)."

Michael Miller: "For several years I would hold a faculty roast at the end of the year for our going away party where I would recognize funny things that each staff member did throughout the year. They would also roast me. Amazing how many (not so bright looking) things I can seem to do throughout the year."

Graham: "Oh my! There are so many experiences that bring laughter for a person in this role. Maintaining a sense of humor is critical to surviving (and thriving) as a principal. One that pops to mind as I type is the first time I sang at a Baccalaureate for a graduating class. It was an arts school, and when the music started the soon-to-be graduates shared an audible gasp as if to say, 'Oh no, our principal thinks she can sing.' (They had no real knowledge of my background in music.) At the end of the song, as they stood to their feet one of the students yelled, 'Hey, my principal can SING!' Both their nervousness for me as well as their appreciation when I finished was as amusing as it was touching."

Pichard: "I had been at a school as principal for about five years and a teacher came into my office, who had been teaching there for a long time. She looked at me and said that there was something different about me. I must have looked puzzled… So she said, 'Oh, I know you shaved off your mustache.' I told her I did not have a mustache or never had one even when I was in college. She left the office. After I got my 'head' back together from the revelation… thinking that this teacher was teaching children and she didn't even realize that I never had a mustache…. I made a mustache out of construction paper and taped it to my upper lip. Then I called in my secretary and had book position so she could not see my fake mustache. I told her the story… then dropped the book. We both had a laugh at the expense of someone's unawareness… but you have to enjoy these moments in the school setting."

Spano: "Going to a school board meeting……………"

Weiss: "During my first year as principal one of my female high school students would have an aggressive outburst towards another female student which usually occurred Friday afternoon. At approximately 2:00 PM, just before we were going to dismiss students to the buses the student began throwing her shoes up on the roof. I asked her if she would step into my office to avoid further problems and I would call her mother to have her picked up so she did not have to ride the bus home. When she came into my office she started cursing and telling me about another student who she was going to fight. I called her mother to come get her. She said she would send the student's grandmother. By now it was just about dismissal time. The grandmother came into my office and very politely escorted her granddaughter to her car. I then started walking towards the buses which were around the building to make sure everyone was dismissed. At about that time an assistant came running down the walkway towards me and said, 'Dr. Weiss, you better get down there fast. There are problems on the bus.' When I got to the bus I found the student and her grandmother trying to start a fight with a student. This student was the one who she had problems with one hour before. At the time it was not so funny but as I told the story to others it really was quite humorous and something for my memoirs."

Gasparino: "I know I have had many humorous situations; I just wished I could remember them!"

Fielding: "If you get a group of principals together socially for ANY activity, it's only a matter of a few minutes before you'll get all the funny stories you could possibly use. Not a day goes by that a teacher doesn't come and share a funny kid story with me. Laughing everyday is what keeps me thinking I'm still young!"

Sanders: "After an over-40 soccer practice, I was pretty dirty and sweaty, and decided to visit the local grocery store. Of course, I ran into one of my students and his parent. I exchanged pleasantries and went about my business. The next day the student told me that after I had left them, his father had remarked, 'No wonder our schools are doing so poorly with principals that look like that!'"

Redd: "Some of the most humerous times having been reading the notes that the parents write when sending their child back to school."

Question: *Share the experience which left a lasting impression.*

Phipps: "I sometimes see students after they have gone on to junior high and high school. I do not see them for years, and then I see them at a game or somewhere. When they come up to me and say, 'Do you remember me? I remember you. You gave me a hug and it made my day.'"

Roy Miller: "The 2nd grader that lost his mother and came to me and spent most of the day 'attached' to my hip when he returned to school. He just wanted to be close and talked when he felt like talking."

Belanger: "When staff members and parents mention how much they appreciate the little things you do, like doing outside duties in the pouring rain or getting to campus long before everyone else. Don't ever ask someone else to do something you would not do."

Mitchell: "This past year we had eleven bomb threats at my school. There were many nasty things being said about the administration, in particular about my incompetence to stop the threats, and my incompetence as a leader. I was at an all time low, but I thought that I was doing a good job covering my feelings with a façade that showed differently. Imagine my spirits soaring when the District Superintendent addressed personnel at a monthly leadership team meeting (includes 87 principals, district senior administrators and other personnel) that he wanted me to know that everyone in the board room and the district supported me, and that I needed to remember that the series of threats had nothing to do with my effectiveness as a principal. I will never forget."

Michael Miller: "I believe loosing a student to a suicide. He had two brothers left in my school and somehow I had to help the faculty and students be able to mourn while at the same time not to dwell on it for the brothers."

Graham: "On September 11, 2001, I had to tell a student that his mother was dead. She was a stewardess on the Pennsylvania flight that crashed that tragic morning."

Pichard: "One that comes to mind is when I lost a staff member to cancer. This teacher was a 'real' teacher. He loved kids. He ate with them at lunch. He communicated with parents. It was very hard to write letters to the parents of his students saying he was going out on medical leave. Then about eight weeks later had to write a letter as a follow up to calling each and every one of the parents of his students that Mr. Bob had passed away. Calling was the best thing… we had a script for all the callers so the same information would be conveyed. Another point is how the staff pulls together to support one another during this time. They expect you as the 'leader' to be there for them and you have to be. They don't prepare you for this in training."

Spano: "The success of a struggling teacher after she followed suggestions made by her support team."

Weiss: "The experience that left a lasting impression occurred when student who was involved in a murder came to school the next day as if nothing had happened."

Gasparino: "The experience that leaves the most lasting impression is whenever a child hugs you and tells you that you're the best principal in the world."

Fielding: "This is sort of like the last question, there are so many. Since this happened about the second year after I came to this school and this is my nineteenth year here, I guess that means it left a lasting impression.

"My school has a population of about 70 percent students who qualify for free or reduced lunch and a mobility rate over 60 percent. I think this is the most fun sort of school to be in, but it does occasionally offer a challenge or two. When I would get a kid in the office, many times for doing something he shouldn't have done, after getting him (or her) calm, I would ask, 'Who do you live with?' I asked that question because many of our students live with grandma, auntie, big brother or some other relative. One day I asked that question to a second grade boy. He gave me kind of a puzzled look and said, 'I don't know.' I know principals who would think the kid was smarting off, but I had learned better. After we talked for a while longer, I found out that he had been in three foster homes in three weeks. The last one dropped him off at school that morning and he truly did not know where he was going after school or who he lived with. He left and I cried, not the first or last time. Since then there have been many experiences, one just this morning, that make me cry."

Sanders: "Last year I had a senior girl, who is also a mom, find out that she had not passed the FCAT which is our high stakes test for graduation. She had all her credits and the GPA that she needed, but would not get her diploma. She cried the entire day."

Redd: "I had a student that was in a wheel chair, and was totally dependant on someone helping him. He used a light ray to help spell things on a board and blinked when trying to spell words on a board. More effort than most kids without disabilities."

Question: *What was your most humbling experience as a principal?*

Phipps: "We had a student that was giving a teacher fits. I was always down there (at teacher's room) with him. This is when I learned, before I lay the bomb down, get the facts. I called the boy's father but he would not come in. The boy's behavior did not get any better so I made a house visit. The boy's mother opened that door and I knew she was sick. She told me she was dying. I went to the school the next day and told the boy's teacher. She's was a mother, so she certainly understood what was going on. We (Phipps and child's teacher) went to the mother's funeral, and you know, that meant so much to that boy. There was another time one child did not want to go home. Finally, I walked the child home because I was worried. We got to his house and there was no electricity, and I mean to tell you it was hot. I tried to pay the electric bill on the phone, but the phone company would not let me. I had to make a mad dash down to the electric company and pay in person. These are the reasons I tell the kids, appreciate everything you have to the fullest."

Roy Miller: "The love that my children show to me for me 'just being me!' "

Belanger: "As a new principal, who don't realize how closely you are watched, by all. You have to watch your tone of voice, your expressions and even how you listen. People, especially staff members, magnify your reactions more closely than any other person on staff. I have had staff ask if I was O.K. because of a small action on my part that I didn't even know I had done."

Mitchell: "I had to learn the hard way that there are times when you cannot trust those who are closest to you, and that others may know more than I do. I had to have one of my assistant principals removed because he was undermining me and my other administrators by reporting to teachers and others (including parents and people in the community) confidential information discussed in closed administration meetings. Much of the information was slanted or untrue. There were many signs — from teachers to parents and students — but I chose to believe that I knew best. Big mistake."

Michael Miller: "Being chosen as the top administrator in my district."

Graham: "Five students overdosed one afternoon at a school where I had been principal only a few short months. (The drug issue was one of several reasons I had been hired to lead there.) The reactions to the anti-depressants the students had taken were as varied as the students themselves. After the initial steps I had to take to deal with the situation were past, I remember sitting in my office and telling God that I finally had come to a place where I really just had no idea what to do. As a 'fix-it' person, one who prided herself on being able to 'problem-solve' just about any situation, this was a very unique place for me to land. I remember being in my office alone asking, 'How do I fix this?' I was thinking of all the great principals I had read about along the way, including Joe Clark, and thought to myself, 'Well, I can't use a baseball bat.' My answer came to me as clearly as if someone else was in the room: 'You're going to fix this one kid at a time.' And, that's just what I – along with others – began to do."

Pichard: "Two years ago I was selected to build a new elementary school. This is an awesome task but was also a humbling experience in thinking you get to pick your staff, purchase all the items from staplers, trash cans, lawn equipment, curriculum items, projectors, computers, etc… with this sum of money. Then put it all together and open the building on time to greet and meet parents and students and start the year off rolling."

Spano: "The death of a staff member."

Weiss: "Probably the most humbling experiences are no matter how much you seen to believe you are helping some children nothing actually changes for them in their lives. It seems like many times we have no control over student outcomes."

Gasparino: "The most humbling experience is when you know that you didn't or couldn't help a child in need."

Fielding: "Well, since the last one was serious, let's make this one funny. When I was transferred to this school one week before teachers came back, I was told I would have 525 kids. When the dust settled on the first day for kids, we had 650. I didn't have rooms or teachers for 125 kids. There was a lady who worked like a maniac all day in the front office, and I didn't even know who she was since she only worked on 'kid days.' I went home and told my wife I'd be surprised if ANYBODY came back to work the next day. Of course they did, we got teacher allocations and hired good teachers and things began to move smoothly. After about a month or so, I figured things were going pretty well and figured I might just get the hang of this principal stuff yet. One of my kindergarten teachers asked me to come read to her class so I picked up 'Leo the Late Bloomer' and went off to read. The kids were all sitting on the rug waiting when I went and sat on the rug in front of them. I was enthusiastically reading along and Leo still wasn't blooming when some kid on the front row says 'Hey Mr. Principal, how come you got on two different shoes?' Well, I looked down and sure enough there was a black one and a brown one. Okay, so maybe I didn't quite have it together yet!

"Of course, humbling experiences are like the funny ones and the ones that make a lasting impression, they happen almost every day. Principals always comment that we should write a book. We'd just have to write the experiences and most people who aren't principals would never believe them.........but, hey, who could make this stuff up?"

Sanders: "I had the local Political cartoonist lampoon me after a very divisive incident occurred at school my first year as principal."

Redd: "Reading books on the roof of an elementary building with a *Cat in the Hat* hat on. (Right to Read Week bet)!"

Question: *Would you share the best joke you've heard about principals and or school administration?*

Belanger: "Quote from Todd Whitaker, 'If a teacher is gone, we call a sub. If a principal is gone, we don't even bother. But if the secretary is gone, we might as well close the school!' "

Mitchell: "True story — when I was an assistant principal at a large high school, my principal gave me a difficult assignment that involved a disgruntled parent and a not so cooperative teacher. I looked at him to ask some questions about the parent, but I guess my eyes were asking something else. My principal leaned his head back as he stood over me and said, 'Just why do you think God made assistant principals?' I laughed so hard! He was actually reading my mind!"

Michael Miller: "I still remember the one about the person not wanting to get out of be and go to school but he had to because he was the Principal. I can identify sometimes."

Graham: "Do people tell jokes about us? Probably one of the best is the person who insists that their son/daughter has to get out of bed and go to school because he/she is the principal."

Weiss: "This is a true story. At a party at the superintendent's home the assistant superintendent decided we should barbecue some steaks. The assistant superintendent (she) asked another administrator and me to accompany her to the supermarket. We were dressed in bathing suits. After choosing the steaks we went to check out. The assistant supeintendent took out her checkbook to pay for the steaks. The cashier asked her for ID which she had left home. The cashier said she could not cash her check without ID. The assistant superentendent said to the cashier, 'Do you see that boy over there? I took him out of Sunland today for a visit (Sunland was an institution for the retarded). He will be very disappointed if we can not have this party.' The cashier looked at the administrator, called over her supervisor, explained the story, and asked the supervisor to approve the check. The supervisor approved the check, and we all left."

Gasparino: "I suppose the best joke would be that we're in it for the money."

Fielding: "I'm not good at remembering jokes, but there have been a million funny stories."

Sanders: Those teachers who complain about their principal being stupid would probably be out of a job if he were any smarter."

Learn From Knowledge

I conversed with Principals Pichard and Fielding on many topics. One of the topics addressed violent acts such as Columbine, and how such acts affect principals personally. I also asked what advice they would give first-year principals when dealing with such heavy responsibility. They, along with other principles, were kind enough to give me detailed feedback on this subject. Here are their comments.

Question: *When considering future, first-year principals, what advice would you give them in dealing with such heavy responsibility (when dealing with violence)?*

Pichard: "I would say to them:

"1) There will be days that you will say, 'Why did I do this?' Yes, there will come a day when you will look into the mirror or say this... but then you will come back to reality and say I am making a difference at this school for students, staff and parents.

"2.) Find a mentor — someone who you can trust so when you have to make some difficult decisions that you and your mentor can discuss and it will stay between you and your mentor. Sometimes talking to the neighboring principal down the street may seem beneficial until others start talking about your situations. Make sure your mentor is someone who you can trust... which takes time and effort of both parties.

"3.) Need to find the positives in every situation or you are going to be consumed with negativity from everyone. Parents will tell you what is wrong with your school while they are there or after they leave, in e-mails or letters. Staff members will tell you how good another school is, but they are not willing to transfer. Students are always looking for something to 'whine about' if it is not meeting their needs. Look for positives... the parents, who support you daily, the teachers who do their job and are happy to be at your school and the students who work hard, obey the rules and do the best they can each day.

"4.) Make sure you juggle time effectively — work and family. This is hard for me to do but I'm trying to do better.

"5.) Don't miss a due date — Make sure you have a good planning system that will work for you so that due dates for reports; memos, etc are not missed."

Fielding: "Hire good staff with common sense and trust that they can handle a crisis. Pay attention when someone brings something unsafe to your attention, even if you think it is nothing. After gathering all the information you can try, as best you can, to not make a mountain out of a mole hill. Most of the time when a parent (it's usually a parent) is telling you about something they think is unsafe, they really just want you to listen. When you need help, don't be afraid to ask or call 911 if necessary. Remember there is a fine line between erring on the side of caution and causing a needless panic."

Question: *How on earth do you (personally) deal with such tremendous responsibility?*

 Pichard: "You can not do it all so these may be a few ways to deal with our job.

"1) **Delegate task**s — Find staff members who want to be more involved in leadership positions, National Board Certified Teachers or teachers just wanting to help make the school 'move' in the right direction. Delegate a task, build in checkpoints for reporting (e-mail is very beneficial this way), have an almost finished checkpoint… just to make sure all puzzle pieces are coming together and then a final report…(before the actual due date just in case you need to finish or polish up a few things).

"2) **Let your staff know** — I try to be transparent with all my staff to let them know as much as I can about items that may impact them. I think this builds a sense of trust and that they know if they come to me with a question they will receive an answer. I have been at some schools as a teacher that sometimes 'teachers' feel like they are the last to know things, which have a tremendous impact on the learning environment of the school. I share budget items, staffing items, vision for the coming year, etc… For Example, right now Florida, there is in a real budget crunch and it is in the newspapers etc… so I try to let the staff know how this will affect our Title I staffing plan and our general staffing plan for teachers. One group of staff members that is often overlooked are the support staff — custodians, cafeteria, teaching assistants and office workers. These folks sometimes hear rumors and then can add to the rumor mill or then become part of the real gossip train in the school.

"I tell my staff that I 'Hate Rumors so if anyone wants to clarify something I am an e-mail, phone call or a visit to my office away. Rumors will kill a school. It creates FEAR = False Education Appearing Real.

"3) **Leadership Committee** — I have a Leadership Committee at my school — members are Assistant Principal, Secretary, Head Custodian, Title I Coordinator, Guidance Counselor, Technology Specialist, Cafeteria Manager, School Age Childcare Coordinator and Reading Coach. We meet every Monday to go over the weekly schedule so that everyone knows exactly what is going on and responsibilities. We also have items listed under each staff member so that we have some target dates of upcoming events, general topics that they are responsible for or other items that they would like to work on. The length of this meeting is no more than 30 minutes if everyone is prepared. We do not discuss each item every week. We highlight the ones needed. Not all of the members attend each week but have an opportunity to attend especially if there is something they would like to bring up, such as the Cafeteria Manager.

"4) **Planbook**, calendar and calendar pad — I use all three to make sure I have a notation of things needed to be completed, reminders...

"**Planbook** — I keep all the memos for things needed to be completed so that I have the original. This helps when we have to send something in and to whom to send it. I place notations in my Planbook about upcoming events based on the dates of the memos... so I have some lead time to get this task delegated or completed.

"School Calendar — Use our school calendar to schedule other events not scheduled as they come up during the year. The school calendar is given to every staff member so they will know events for the year… ahead of time. However, just because it is on the calendar does not mean it will happen, but 99 percent do. Such things on the staff calendar will be Awards Days, Fire Drills, End of the grading periods, etc.

"Calendar Pad — Use my little calendar flip pad on my desk to remind me of things to do, office staff who will be out, etc. This is my memory 'trigger' just so I will know at a glance of who may be out or when I need to send something out via e-mail or when something is due.

"All three of these working together may seem redundant but checks and balances will keep you from being called by the district office asking you where 'such and such' is that was due last week."

Fielding: (In reference to violence in the schools) "I try to follow my own advice from #1. Pray a lot and trust in God's plan."

Question: *When these incidents occur at other schools (in reference to Columbine), what emotions do you experience?*

Prichard: "I think about the phrase – 'Any given day' someone could come into ANY school in ANY city or small town, and change the way things are done from that moment forward if they want to. I look at the United States Capital…where a gunman got through all the detectors and shot up the capital a few years ago killing a Capital policemen. Of course, all the school tragedies shed some light on how prepared you and your staff are for this type of event. The scary thing is you will never know until it really happens. You can have the best laid plans and when it 'breaks lose' you have to make sure that people are doing what they need to be doing and those not doing it need to be replaced by someone who can do the job when emotions run high in panic situations. Whenever an incident happens I always make sure my staff receives an e-mail or we discuss it at the next faculty meeting...the specifics of the incident and how vulnerable we are at a school.

"Also when I hear a report about a school incident I always say a prayer for that principal, staff members, students, parents and community because now that community has been changed forever by one incident; whether it be a school shooting, fire, when the hurricanes of a few years ago destroyed and damaged neighboring county schools, a staff member arrested, and the list goes on and on."

Fielding: "If you're familiar with the MBTI, I'm an ESTP, so I tend to be practical, sometimes to a fault according to my wife. When some catastrophe hits the news, I tend to first think of how to manage the fallout of people questioning the safety of their kids. Then I slow down and empathize with the principals, staff, students and families involved."

Straight From the Veterans

In speaking with these principals I have come to the conclusion that finding veteran principals who are excellent leaders is like finding a treasure trove. They determine the future of our children, and our children determine our future. By having school districts and state leaders, such as former Governor James Hunt, take steps to assure that our principals will be great leaders, they are taking steps to guarantee we will continue to have our freedoms in a unique country.

With these thoughts on how you play a part in our future, I will leave you with more words of wisdom from our veteran principals. I asked each principal if they had other words of encouragement, advice, information, or a personal story to pass on to you. Here is what they had to say:

Roy Miller: "It is a rewarding job. However, it is a job that takes a lot of time. You spend an enormous amount of time before and after school. You will have weekends when you must take things home. You will find yourself in the lives of your faculty. You will become their counselor in many ways. You must take time to 'listen.' Also, I learned a long time ago that if they come to complain, they must also come with a solution where their complaint is concerned. If not, I just listen and say 'thank you.' "

Belanger: "The best advice I can offer is to find a group of other principals you can use as your sounding board, to share experiences and gain knowledge. Meeting once a month with the group I am with has given me the feeling that I am not in this alone and that I need to trust my decisions. Principals need to remember to not forget their families and make sure to have a balance between your professional and private lives."

Michael Miller: "This is the most unrealistic job I have ever had with the demands, and what I am responsible for, that I have no say so in, but it also the most rewarding I have every had. I had the opportunity to take a school from the bottom to the top. Test scores and morale were the lowest ever when I arrived and now we are a model school that has achieved great scores and at the same time my teachers are happy. We work hard but we play hard also."

Pichard: "Go to work with a smile. Be out and about in your building. Work hard. Be Professional. Get a good support team of fellow principals to call.

"Have fun everyday. Make sure you take time for yourself. Remember that TODAY IS THE BEST IT IS GOING TO BE.

"Tomorrow is another day and you will get up and do it all over again knowing that TODAY IS THE BEST IT IS GOING TO BE."

What Makes a Great Principal

After interviewing some outstanding leaders and doing research for *Your First Year as a Principal*, it became obvious what makes a principal a truly wonderful principal. You must be proficient in many areas, good with people, a leader with vision and goals, but more importantly, you must have heart and broad shoulders with which to help those who come to you. As Oliver Phipps said in regards to hiring new teachers, "Look for the heart."

It is important to leave you with some words from Principal Fielding, a phenomenal principal with a sense of humor, a sense of integrity, a set of shoulders with which he carries much responsibility and caring, and a man with a heart. What you are about to read is the first part of Principal Fielding's teacher handbook. You will see exactly what makes this man an exceptional principal for his staff, his teachers, parents, community, and his numerous students. For all first-year principals, now and those to come, our children will flourish and be kept in good hands if you learn from the words of the great principals you have read about in *Your First Year as a Principal*. Even though nothing can better train you than personal, hands-on experience, nothing can better prepare you than the wisdom of those who have been there before you.

From the *Teacher Handbook* by Dr. John Fielding, Principal of Idylwild Elementary School.

Beginning Stuff

"If you have ever been through a full interview with me, you know that I always give you a chance to ask anything you want. Most people, and everybody I've hired, have questions. Probably the most frequent is some version of 'What do you look for in teachers?' While the specific words of my answer probably change, the basic philosophy doesn't. The short answer is that I look for someone who can do whatever job I'm interviewing you for better than I can, then try my best to give you what you need to be successful and get out of the way. The next few paragraphs are the longer version of that answer.

"I believe that it is important for you to understand that you have chosen what I believe is the **most important profession** of all. The Teacher Perceiver Inventory defines 'mission' as 'a deep underlying belief that students can grow and attain self-actualization. A teacher with mission has a goal to make a significant contribution to other people.' When I look for teachers, I look first for someone who displays a strong sense of mission. You must really believe in your heart that you are the most important person in changing a child, any child, into a productive adult. Any teacher who does not proudly display that belief should be selling shoes. My job as principal is to take teachers with mission and provide you with every possible resource to help you fulfill your mission.

"One question on the TPI asks you to tell me what you believe an ideal school would be like. I think it is only fair that you know what I believe an ideal school would be like. In my ideal school everyone, from the youngest child to the oldest staff member, would be treated the same way you and I would like to be treated. Each person would be positive, encouraging and empathetic with every other person. Everyone would feel successful in some way at the end of each day. Teachers would find ways to make each child believe that he or she was 'teacher's pet.' Teachers would constantly be looking for innovative ways to challenge students.

They would always be trying to learn something new to improve their ability to help others both personally and professionally. Everyone would understand that listening skills are important and that you determine if you have been a good listener by looking to see if the speaker has been helped. Every teacher, every day, would be excited, not because they had done a good job of teaching, but because they had seen 'a light come on' in each child. Every teacher would understand that even tiny little successes are important and learn to build on them. Everyone would actively seek to build rapport with everyone else. Parents would be welcome and would look forward to coming to school.

"If you have read carefully you should have noticed that the most important things in my ideal school are relationships. Does that mean that I don't value good teaching, a strong, relevant curriculum, lots of resources and pleasant surroundings? Of course not. However, I don't believe any of those things are possible without the positive relationships being in place first. Many of us have our own kids. You know the kinds of things you want them to learn. You want them to know how to get along with other people as well as all of the 'book learning' that they will get in school. Each of you has an important role to play in helping our Idylwild kids learn to get along with others. Kids learn by watching adults. When they see you being helpful, kind and courteous, they will model helpful, kind and courteous behavior. If you allow your frustration to show and "act out," they will model that too.

"I invite you to share my vision of an ideal school by working first and hardest on building a strong positive rapport with every student, each other, other staff members and parents.

"Some of you may now be thinking 'Okay, so what does he really want?' There is a quote by Donald Murray in the book, *In The Middle*, which answers that question for me.

'What do you want, they keep asking me...I want them to do what I do not expect them to do, and if they do not do what I do not expect them to do I must be failing somewhere.'

"I first read, and reread that quote many years ago. The more I thought about it the more I realized what it meant for me. I evaluate myself on how much you go 'beyond the call of duty' and do things for kids and each other that I have no right to 'expect' you to do. You might think about that in your relationships with your kids."

BIBLIOGRAPHY

Lew Armistead, *"Public Relations and the High School Principal."* Spring 2007, **<http://www.principalspartnership.com/feature1003.html>** (28 February 2008).

Jan Baumel, *"Understanding Special Education Laws and Rights,"* Great Schools Inc., 9 June 2006, **<http://www.schwablearning.org/articles. aspx?r=78>** (12 March 2008).

Abby Barry Bergman. *A Survival Kit for the Elementary School Principal: With Reproducible Forms, Checklists, and Letters, Paramus,* Prentice Hall, 1998.

Barbara L. Brock and Marilyn L. Grady, *Launching Your First Principalship: A Guide for Beginning Principals.* Thousand Oaks: Corwin Press, 2004.

Cathy Cravits, *"Do You Have What it Takes To Be a School Principal?"* EZine Articles, 21 September 2007, **<http://ezinearticles.com>** (17 April 2008).

Philip A.Cusick, *"A Study of Michigan's School Principal Shortage,"* Michigan StateUniversity, N.D. **<http//www.epc.msu.edu/publications/REPORT/ REPORT.pdf>** (20 April 2008).

Richard A.DiPatri, *"In Brevard Public Schools, The People Make the Difference,"* February 2008, **<http://www.brevard.k12.fl.us>** (14 April 2008).

Edmonton Catholic School District, *"Dealing With Parent – School Conflict Management,"* 2008, **<http://www.ecsd.net/parents/conflict_ managment.html>** (27 March 2008).

Good Shepherd Catholic School, *"General Info, Principal,"* 2007, **<http//. www.gsschool.org/general_principal.html>** (07 April 2008).

Bridget Gutierrez, *"Principals: How Important Are They?"* The Atalantic Journal-Constitution, 27 November 2007, **<http://www.aja.com/blogs>** (18 April 2008).

Cassandra Hopkins, *"Principal's Message,"* Rivers Edge Elementary School, N. D., **<http://www.clayton.k12.ga.us/schools/129/principal.html>** (8 March 2008).

Gary Hopkins, *"The Best and Worst Things About Being a Principal,"* Education World, 2001, **<http://www.educationworld.com/a_admin/ admin/admin253.shtml>** (12 March 2008).

Stacey Marlow and Norman Minehira, *"Principals as Curriculum Leaders: New Perspectives for the 21st Century,"* Pacific Resources for Education and Learning, N.D., **<http://www.prel.org/products/Products/Curriculum. htm>** (15 February 2008).

National Association of Elementary School Principals, *"Vision 2021,"* NAESP ONLINE, Spring 2007, **<http://www.vision2021.org/ anticipating_the_future_.html>** (7 April 2008).

The Ohio Association of Elementary School Administrators, "*OAESA Mission,*" OAESA Brochure, N.D., **<http://www.oaesa.org/brochures/whome.pdf>** (1April 2008).

The Ohio Association of Secondary School Administrators, "*OASSA Mission,*" OASSA Update, August 2004, **<htt://www.oassa.org/>** (4 April 2008).

John Arul Philips, "*Manager – Administrator to Instructional Leader: Shift in the Role of School Principal,*" Faculty of Education, Universtiy of Malaya, N.D., **<http://www.peoplelearn.homestead.com/principainstructleader.htm>** (3 March 2008).

Robert Ricken and Michael Terc and Ida Ayres, "*The Elementary School Principals Calendar: A Month-by-Month Planner For the School Year,*" Thousand Oaks, Corwin Press, 2006.

Grace Rubenstein, "*Pyzant on Principals: Key Players in School Reform,*" Edutopia, June 2006, **<http://www.edutopia.org/payzant-principals>** (4 April 2008).

Laurel L. Schmidt, "*Gardening in the Minefield: A Survival Guide for School Administrators,*" Portsmouth, Heinemann, 2002.

Mark Wagner, "*Yet Another Blog,*" 26 August 2007, **<http://www.decimation.com/markw/2007/08/26/how-to-fire-a-teacher>** (9 March 2008).

Todd Whitaker, *What Great Principals Do Differently: Fifteen Things That Matter Most,* Larchmont, EYE on Education, 2003.

Wikimedia Foundation, "*United States Department of Education,*" Wikipedia, 2 April 2008, **<http://www.en.wikipedia.org/wiki/United_States_Department_of_Education>** (8 April 2008).

Priscilla Wohlsletter and Susan Albers Mohrmon, *"School-Based Management: Strategies for Success,"* PRE Publications, January 1993, **<http://www.ed.gov./pubs/CPRE/fb2sbm.html>** (12 April 2008).

Susan Tave Zelman, Superintendent of Public Instruction, *"Entry Year Principals and Mentoring Component,"* 25 June 2007, **<http://www.ode. state.oh.us/>** (30 February 2008).

AUTHOR BIOGRAPHY

––––––

At the age of nine Tena Green discovered a great escape through *Treasure Island*, which hooked her on reading forever. With insightful encouragement from her sixth grade teacher, Mr. Walker, she started writing for pleasure at age eleven. Being a shy, timid young girl she moved many times while growing up, which is how reading and writing became not only her getaway, but her passion.

Green volunteered in the schools for several years before becoming a substitute secretary, a teacher's aide, and intervention specialist. In 2001 she took a journalist position for a local newspaper and started doing freelance. Less than two years after starting as a journalist she published her first novel, *The Catalyst* (2003), and has since written *A Woman's Touch* (2006) and *X-30* (2007), a collaboration with friend and horror writer, Richard Dean.

Green is still writing novels, giving school presentations on how to use reading and writing as an outlet, working as an editor for author-me.com, and writing freelance articles. According to Green the greatest benefit to come from her writing has been all the wonderful people she has come to know. You may contact Green through her website at **www.tenagreen. com.**

INDEX
